# A KINDLE IN THE KINGDOM

*Christian Missions Strategy in the Caribbean*

DR. RANDOLPH WALTERS

**Written and Created By:** Dr. Randolph Walters

**Published by:** Jabez Publishing House

**Designed by:** J. Michael Advertising

**Copyright Disclaimer**

"Why is it that some Christians cross land and sea, continents and cultures, as missionaries? What on earth impels them? It is not in order to commend a civilization, an institution or an ideology, but rather a person, Jesus Christ, whom they believe to be unique." - John R.W. Stott

# Praise for

# A Kindle in the Kingdom

If you have ever wondered how the Holiness movement spread in the Caribbean, this is your book. In fact, there is simply no other history of the Holiness Church that outlines both the cultural dynamism and tensive developments that inform both its North American and Caribbean Roots. Dr. Randolph Walters' *A KINDLE IN THE KINGDOM* brings order to a massively complicated subject and provides the reader an opportunity to interpret why certain events and phenomena mark important distinctions in the outworking of Protestant Christianity in the Caribbean context. Dr. Walters reveals how modern "pilgrims" wrestled with some of the great and formative questions of the Christian faith, such as spiritual formation, the true meaning of conversion and evangelism. These issues were defined in the crucible of cultural change, political recomposition, spiritual leadership and theological controversy, all set against the background of the postcolonial world. Dr. Walters› highly accessible style shows that theology and biblical appropriation in the service of evangelization/evangelism and mission was a spiritual endeavor woven into the texture of the Holiness narrative in the Caribbean. Finally, this book makes a potent argument that the Holiness movement should be understood as an independent force, one that developed a life of its own, often exercising a decisive influence, not only upon the history of missions, but on nation-building, social emancipation and the practice of inculturation. Dr. Walters' accessible volume is a much needed corrective to Christian ignorance and suspicion of a central modern movement, combatting the claim that the faith and practice of the Holiness movement is divergent from missional activity and foreign to evangelism. *A Kindle in the Kingdom* will be read and appreciated by scholars across academic disciplines.

**Dr. Adetokunbo Adelekan**
Associate Professor of Theology and Ethics
Palmer Theological Seminary of Eastern University
Senior Pastor, Tabernacle Baptist Church, Dayton, Ohio
Author of *"A Charge to Keep: Re-Missioning the Urban Church for the 21st Century"*

# Praise for

# A Kindle in the Kingdom

Dr. Walters' book, *A Kindle in the Kingdom: Christian Missions Strategy in The Caribbean* is a very readable attention-grabbing book that tells the story of Wesleyan Holiness and Pentecostal missions' influence on the shape of Christianity in the Caribbean and in Barbados in particular. By looking at the historical roots of these movements, Dr. Walters demonstrates the interconnectedness of revivals among nations and how Caribbean cultures were ripe for the soul-stirring tone of the Great Awakenings. At the same time, Dr. Walters makes clear that Christian missions in Barbados illustrate how indigenous cultures shape the reception of Christian missionary efforts, which is an invaluable lesson in contextual missiology. As a theologian, I welcome Dr. Walters' exploration of the relationships among Wesleyan theologies of sanctification for his nuancing of distinctive strains within the Holiness and Pentecostal "traditions." Dr. Walters adds here to the growing body of literature that discerns cultural contributions to Christian faith and practice beyond the European colonial contexts. His is a valuable addition to this larger story.

**Donald James Brash, Ph.D.**
Associate Professor of Historical Theology
Faculty Director of the Doctor of Ministry Program
Palmer Theological Seminary of Eastern University

Dr. Walters presents an historical and theological journey of faith from Methodism to Holiness in the Caribbean. Whether a student of missions or spiritual movements, this is worth a read to understand the intersection of culture, religion and global missions.

**Dr. J. Nathan Corbitt**
Emeritus Professor of Cross-Cultural Studies
Eastern University
Author of "*The Sound of the Harvest: Music's Mission in Church and Culture*"

# Contents

# DEDICATION

To my mother and maternal grandmother, your inspiration and encouragement were instrumental in shaping the formative years of my faith and you helped give me a love for God's Word.

To Pastor Ernest Morris, my first Pastor, thanks for modeling what it meant to be a servant sold out to Christ. You provided the DNA for my missions' sensibilities.

To all the spiritual leaders and men and women of faith whose lives have inspired and encouraged me to live on mission.

# ACKNOWLEDGEMENTS

I n a book about Missions, I am deeply grateful to two men who stood with me during the early stages of conception of this missions research – renowned missiologist Dr. Samuel Escobar and expert in Historical Theology, Dr. Horace Russell. Their encouragement and expertise were invaluable.

My thanks to Pastor James Bend, Rev. Dr. Noel Titus, Dr. John Gilmore, Rev. Carlisle Williams of Barbados, and the various members of the Wesleyan Holiness Church in Barbados for their personal interviews in 1996.

Thanks to my wife Betty, a true companion, faithful woman of God, and intercessor. She continues to give me both the space to be on mission and the privilege to be partnered in mission.

# FOREWORD

Current Caribbean church historians and missiologists have a difficult task. On the one hand there are subject to the pressures from Caribbean churches for an authentic word from them about the past and some information of the journey into the present. At the same time there are also competing voices from outside the church communities with varying agendas, some religious, and others not using the same or similar sources to present their competing narratives. This was because until recently it was accepted that the historical archives of Europe and in some instances the United States were more authentic than the oral testimonies of the Caribbean people among whom they lived. Gladly those days are on the wane and one can only hope that in the expanded market place of ideas more nuggets of truth may be discovered and more adequate expressions of the real happenings emerge. It is this task that Prof. Randolph Walters, a Barbadian Christian scholar has undertaken in **A Kindle in the Kingdom: Christian Missions Strategy in the Caribbean**.

For many decades Caribbean church historians and missiologists have been engaged in examining the ways by which the Gospel became a liberating agent to the enslaved in the region and how it severed the bonds of European colonization. This meant for the most part an evaluation of the missionary movement of the 19th century and its ambivalence to both slavery and colonialism. Somewhat later this was followed with the scholarly examination of the religious life of the slaves themselves through the lens of sociology and anthropology. These findings at times conflicted with the conclusions drawn by church historians and missiologists who had only the European governments, missionary and colonial archives to consult with their obvious biases. Happily the situation has changed and there is a determined effort to find the areas of agreement and differences. Even so the apparent syncretism and /or indigenization which occurred when the complex of European Christian beliefs and practices encountered the varied African religious beliefs and practices still have not yet been fully documented or interpreted. Sadly the same is true as regards the study of Asian religious beliefs and their impact on the Caribbean.

**A Kindle in the Kingdom: Christian Missions Strategy in the Caribbean** is therefore a welcomed addition to the current dialogues in search of Caribbean Christian origins and especially with its examination of the neglected subject of **holiness**. This book is a prism through which we might observe an aspect of Caribbean church life as it is practiced and lived today. Apart from the general studies of Pentecostalism and the Revival movements and even within them the quest for Holiness or Sanctification as a sine qua non is often absent. Yet it was this quest for the sanctified life stimulated by the witness of members of T**he Church of the Brethren** (the Moravians) which inspired John Wesley, the founder of Methodism moving him to a deeper faith commitment, and also others like the Countess of Huntingdon and her Connection. Similarly this desire for a holy life led to the devotional writings of Hannah More, *Thoughts on the influence of Manners of the Court to General Society* (1788), *Practical Piety* (1811), and William Wilberforce, *Real Christianity* (1797),**Practical view of Prevailing Religious System of Professed Christians contrasted with Real Christianity** (1811) and to the hymns of Charles Wesley, **I want a principle within** (1749), **Come Holy Ghost our souls inspire** (1740), James Montgomery, **Prayer is the souls sincere desire** (1818), and John Newton, **Amazing Grace** (1772). The search for the sanctified life undergirded the Evangelical Movement and might even be trace back to Jonathan Edwards and was constitutive of the zeal expressed in the Awakenings by preachers like Charles Finney and

Dwight L. Moody in the United States and seen also in the Revivals it stimulated in the United Kingdom. The search for the 'life of holiness' undergirds movements like the Salvation Army, Keswick and the current Holiness and Pentecostalist Churches of Barbados and the Caribbean, the subject of this missiological study.

Too often have Christians forgotten at their peril that the invitation of the Gospel is to a way of life which not only embraces but also rejects. In the embrace of the Good News there is a call to be open to be more like Jesus Christ. It is the call to be holy as He is holy. This is not easy but it is a journey that each Christian is called to make and Prof. Randolph Walters in **A Kindle in the Kingdom: Christian Missions Strategy in the Caribbean** invites challenges and encourages not only Caribbean Christians but the church catholic to such an endeavor.

**Rev. Dr. Horace O. Russell**
Emeritus Professor of Historical Theology and Dean of Chapel
Palmer Theological Seminary of Eastern University
Retired Pastor of the Saints Memorial Baptist
Church in Bryn Mawr, Pennsylvania
Author of *"Ten Reasons For Living: Studies in the Lord's Prayer"*

# INTRODUCTION

The Wesleyan Holiness Church of Barbados is over one hundred years old and has become one of the leading Evangelical Churches on the island. It has existed alongside the Methodist Church with which it shares a common source and much of its theological perspective. This significant relationship lies in the united emphasis on the Wesleyan doctrine of sanctification.

In the 19th century, the Holiness Movement grew out of an attempt to revitalize Methodism. American Methodism, in particular, had become very sensitive to the protests which emerged from the camp meetings and very responsive to the revivalism consequent on the Second Great Awakening. At the same time, British Methodism was also influenced by the influx and visits of American evangelists, particularly Charles G. Finney and his theological and methodological emphases. Both these influences had their impact upon Caribbean Methodism, which had become firmly established by the end of the 18th century, and upon the development of Holiness Churches. In Barbados, these Holiness Churches were a result of North American missions which had entered during the early part of the 20th century. Indeed, these churches were products of a spiritual awakening, which during the previous half-century had cultivated among many denominations the doctrine and influence of Christian perfection or entire sanctification.

Contemporaneous with the Holiness Movement was also the Pentecostal Movement with its origins in Azusa Street in the United States. The major characteristics of the Holiness movement were not only inherited, but perpetuated by the Pentecostal Movement. In the early period, except for the issue of "speaking in tongues," there was little to distinguish a Pentecostal believer from a Holiness believer.

The task of this book is to discover what were the sources of the Holiness Movement in the English-speaking Caribbean in general and Barbados in particular. The book reveals how the Holiness Movement propagated itself at the turn of the 20th century and it develops some lessons for missionary strategy and theological reflection in our time.

The book contains the following:

1. A survey of the origins of the Holiness Movement in the United States and in Britain.

2. An examination of the relationship of the Holiness Movement to its parent churches in Barbados.

3. An examination of the work of the Methodist Missionary Society in Barbados and the growth of the Wesleyan Holiness Church.

4. An examination of how the early missionaries institutionalize their responses to get the message of Holiness across, as well as the relationship with Pentecostalism in Barbados.

5. A discussion of some lessons derived from the establishment and growth of the Wesleyan Holiness Church for the Church and Society in Barbados, and for Caribbean Missions and theology.

# CHAPTER ONE

# BARBADOS: A GENERAL OVERVIEW

All societies have been shaped by geography and history. Barbados is no exception, and, as in all societies, the impact of geography and history on Barbados, and indeed the Caribbean in general, has been unique. Any attempt to examine and understand that society as it stands today must be founded on an appreciation of this cardinal truth. It is against this background that I present a brief history of Barbados as a frame of reference for my discussion of the Wesleyan Holiness Church.

Barbados is the most easterly of the Caribbean islands. It lies to the southeastern corner of the group of islands known as the Windward Islands; it is ninety miles from its nearest neighbor. This beautiful "island in the sun" is twenty-one miles long with a breadth of fourteen miles at the widest place. It has an area of 166 square miles and is divided into eleven parishes. A "parish" is a sub-region akin to a state in the American context. Each parish has its own features and physical attractions. The term parish has its origins in the Anglican Church of England. Historically, the Anglican Church has been the dominant church in Barbados because of the island's English settlement in 1627.

Barbados was the last of the islands to be settled by Europeans, for Columbus' ships seemed to have passed it without notice during the early Spanish settlement in the 15th century. At the time of settlement, few ships passed near it. It is believed that the island was visited by the Portuguese in the early part of the 16th Century, and to them it owes its name "Los Barbados," the isle of the bearded trees. Despite the Portuguese visit, the island remained unsettled by Europeans for a century after. In 1624, John Powell claimed Barbados for England. John Powell had been trading with Brazil and came upon Barbados by chance. It seemed a suitable island to claim for King James I, and Powell returned in 1627 with his brother Henry Powell and a substantial number of settlers. Barbados was therefore settled by the British in 1627 and unlike many of the other islands, remained British throughout the colonial period until its Independence from Britain in November 1966. The British influence is therefore very evident in the institutions and culture of Barbadian society. Barbados was also the most densely populated island in the Caribbean.

In the early period, Barbados, like the other islands, concentrated on producing tobacco for export to England and Europe. However, by the end of the 1630's tobacco growers were met with serious competition from Virginian tobacco, and falling profits forced planters to search for an alternative crop. The result was a rapid and dramatic changeover to the production of sugar. King Sugar dominated the economy and had significant consequences for the demographic, social and economic structure of the island. Nothing was more important to the sugar plantations than a large labor force of African slaves. As a result, the society became predominantly African in terms of numbers. This demographic reality is evident in contemporary Barbadian Society where over 92 percent of the population is of African descent. Sugar has always been an important aspect of Barbadian life. By the mid-1970's, sugar and its by-products still accounted for the bulk of Barbados' exports. Today, it has given way to tourism, offshore finance, light industry and information services as the leading foreign exchange earners.

As a British colony, Barbados developed a system of government based on the British tripartite system. In the colonial period, the Old Representative System which existed consisted of a Governor, Council and Assembly (made up of wealthy

3

planters). Barbados never lost the Assembly which Charles I granted in 1639. Barbados can therefore boast as having one of the oldest Parliaments in the Commonwealth, and indeed the Western Hemisphere. Barbados secured Ministerial government in 1954, self-government in 1961 and Independence in 1966, reflecting a long history of Parliamentary institutions. Following Independence, Barbados remained a Constitutional Monarchy with a Governor-General as Head of State in a symbolic and ceremonial office as the Queen's Representative.

In terms of missionary activity, the Anglican Church (Church of England) was taken for granted as the official church. This was true of all British colonies, for by the 18th Century it was firmly established in England as the official church. The Anglican Church dominated the religious activity of the island in the early period with a few churches in each parish. The Anglican Church had almost unchallenged responsibility for Church life in the British West Indies; however, the Church was more popular with the merchants and planters than with the slaves, to whose sufferings it often seemed to show indifference.

In Britain more radical groups wanted a more active religion, one that was more responsive to social injustices. As a result, several of these groups began to show a particular interest in the welfare of African slaves. Their first concern was to teach the Christianity which the Anglican Church often seemed to neglect. Contact with the slaves made them sympathetic to the slaves' condition, and this inspired a deep suspicion in the planters that the missionaries were trying to undermine the slave system.

Before 1815, however, missionary activity in the West Indies was only on a small scale. The Society for the Propagation of the Gospel in Foreign Parts was founded in 1701. Its task was to spread Church of England teaching. Only in Barbados was there any real impact, for a bequest by Christopher Codrington, once Governor of the Leeward Islands, enabled the Society to set up Codrington College in 1733. Today this remains one of the leading theological Seminaries in the Caribbean and is a home for the training of Anglican and other clergy. At the end of the 18th Century, the Church of England set up another Society for the Conversion of Negro Slaves. By this time, however, other groups were in the mission field, especially the Moravians, who sought to teach Christian morality by example. Credit for the beginning of Protestant missionary work in the islands must go to the Moravians. The Moravians arrived in Barbados in 1765; by 1788, a Methodist mission was formally established in Barbados. Barbados attracted the attention of the Salvation Army in 1892, and in 1897 the African Methodist Episcopal Church was established. By the turn of the 20th Century several North American missions entered Barbados, each establishing their brand of Christianity. All products of the Holiness revival in North America, they emphasized holiness in Christian living. The Pilgrim (Wesleyan) Holiness Church 1911; Church of God (Anderson)1912; New Testament Church of God 1917; and the Church of the Nazarene 1926 are all examples of these missions. By the 20th Century, therefore, Barbados became a mission field for North American revivalists and Holiness missionaries.

In the United States, one would not find the term "Anglican church" in use. It should be noted that the Episcopal Church is the American branch of the worldwide Anglican Communion. This makes sense since the history of the United States began as a history of English settlers. A common reality in colonization and migration history globally, is the praxis of the colonizer or migrant bringing their religion with them. This was certainly true of the first settlers to the United States. In the first English colony at Jamestown, there were of course Anglicans. After the long and hard struggle of the American Revolution, the English settlers who remained in the United States changed the name of their now "American-based" church to the "Protestant" Episcopal Church of the U.S.A. This was an attempt to distinguish the Episcopal Church from the Roman Catholic Church, as well as a reflection of decolonization. In a free and post-Revolutionary America, the idea of the Anglican Church being a state church with the King of England being the secular head was not an attractive or favorable idea. Those Anglicans then "were not feeling it." At the time, there was a need for reorganization. However, institutions often have a way of moving on from the past. Anglicans in the United States certainly did, and today the Episcopal Church U.S.A is now fully "in communion" with the Church of England, as well as with other Anglican churches throughout the world.

# CHAPTER TWO

# THE DEVELOPMENT OF THE HOLINESS MOVEMENT IN THE UNITED STATES

Before one attempts to survey the Holiness movement in the United States and Britain, it is helpful to put it in theological perspective. When we speak of the "Holiness Movement," we refer to those churches, associations, or groups who teach that entire sanctification is to be received as a second work of grace subsequent to regeneration. We exclude from the term those groups who believe that speaking in tongues is the evidence of having received the baptism with the Spirit, and those persons who do not believe that sin is actually cleansed from the heart of the believer. What is interesting about the first group of "excluders" is that it is made up of Pentecostals, a group that owes its inspiration and formation to the Holiness revival of the 19th Century. R.M. Anderson in *Vision of the Disinherited: The Making of American Pentecostalism* made this same connection between the Pentecostal movement and the Holiness movement. He argued that:

> "Initially a faction within the Holiness camp, the Pentecostal movement drew much of its membership and nearly all of its leadership from Holiness ranks."[1]

It is therefore important to recognize that any attempt to examine and discuss the Holiness movement must involve at the same time reference to the concept of Pentecostalism. The Holiness Movement cannot be therefore seen in isolation, and this is evident in the following discussion.

It is also important at the outset to point out that the Name of John Wesley is forever linked with the doctrine of Holiness or entire sanctification. It was through Wesley that the experience of sanctification was brought into clear light to many believers. This precipitated a renewal revival. Under Wesley, the Methodist Church developed and out of that the various groups that teach Holiness. Holiness churches therefore hold firmly to John Wesley's position on sanctification.

Denominations like the Free Methodists, the Wesleyan Methodists, and the Nazarenes came into being in the 19th

---

[1]  R.M. Anderson. <u>Vision of the Disinherited: The Making of American Pentecostalism.</u> New York: Oxford University Press, 1979, 28.

Century to embody the Wesleyan concern for sanctification. The following examples reflect similar teachings which had grown elsewhere:

I.    With Charles G. Finney, who stressed the possibility for Christians going to a higher, more refined plane of spirituality.

II.   In the Salvation Army.

III.  In certain branches among the Quakers.

IV.   In the Keswick Movement with its stress on the higher Christian life. These will be discussed further.

## HOLINESS BEFORE WESLEY'S TIME

The student of Church history will quickly recognize that the doctrine of Holiness or perfection took many forms throughout the history of the Church. In the Old Testament it seems clear that even in ritual matters of Mosaic religion, God sought to inculcate in the hearts of His people the idea of His holiness and of His claims on men. In the New Testament, this teaching becomes specific. Holiness is now held forth not merely as a standard, but as a glorious possibility through the atoning work of Christ. In the book of Acts and in the Pauline Epistles the experience of Holiness seems to reach its fullest announcement. The baptism of the Holy Spirit recorded in Acts chapter two transformed the church into a vibrant missionary force. Careful reading of the Pauline and General Epistles reveal the writers describing an experience referred to variously as "holiness," "sanctification," "being filled with the Spirit," "perfect love," or "perfection" (Romans 6, Romans 8, 1 Corinthians 6:11, Ephesians 4:24., 1 Thessalonians 4:3-5, 1 John 2:5, 1 John 4:18). The call to some new level of grace is clearly evident.

The writer of Luke-Acts preserves indications of a deeper life in two ways:

I.  There are references to the continuing privilege of receiving the Spirit (Acts 1:4, Acts 2:4, 38).

II.  This was accomplished by the laying on of hands and gave rise to the ritual of confirmation (Acts 19:6, Acts 8:17).

In addition to this tradition, the ideal of a higher life was also emphasized in the Medieval period.

As we move to the Reformation, the doctrine of Holiness is not lost. The leaders of the Reformation have not usually been thought of as teaching a standard of Holiness. Their task was that of reasserting the doctrine of justification by faith and the right of each Christian to come personally to God. However, it can be pointed out that there is, in Martin Luther's writings, some indications of such a standard of life. Soon after the Reformation, certain groups began to lay the foundations which led directly to the teaching of Wesley. Two of these groups should be noted especially. The work of James Arminius and his followers in Holland gave rise to a teaching known as Arminianism. Arminianism focused on the free will of human beings, and God's prevenient grace and sovereignty in relation to salvation. This tradition was transplanted to England and became one of the streams of teaching within the Anglican Church. Wesley's doctrine as later developed was definitely Arminian.

The aim of the preceding discussion is to put two things in perspective:

I.   The doctrine of Holiness as a scriptural doctrine.
II.  The recognition that the doctrine did not originate with John Wesley.

However, Wesley had a great part to play historically in its development and statement. His work is very closely related to the entire modern Holiness Movement. Given the importance of John Wesley's work, a brief look at him is imperative.

## JOHN WESLEY: A BRIEF SKETCH

John Wesley was born in England on June 17, 1703 and died on March 2, 1791. Wesley came from a family that had been identified with the work of the Church. His great-grandfather,

Bartholomew Wesley, was a rector in the established Church and was later ejected as a Puritan. His grandfather, John Wesley, preached as a Nonconformist minister at Whitchurch. Wesley was therefore born in a home of piety. His Father, Samuel Wesley, was the rector of the Church at Epworth. His mother, Susannah Wesley, was a woman of strong religious devotion and raised her family along lines of strict piety.

In 1725, a great increase in Wesley's desire for spiritual experiences became evident. In September of that year, at the age of 22, he preached his first sermon. From this time on, for several years, his life was marked by a constant search for peace with God and for the means of attaining a holy life. It is during this period that a group at Oxford joined together in a band for spiritual profit. They were nicknamed Methodists from whence the name was later transferred to Wesley's converts. Wesley gave a clear doctrinal statement regarding the doctrine of entire sanctification. The Wesleyan revival gave the doctrine a force that spread it abroad. Out of the revival grew the Methodist Movement that kept alive the doctrine of Holiness, which Wesley claimed the Methodists had been raised up by God to spread abroad.

When the Methodists later tended to neglect or to reinterpret the doctrine, there arose some new churches or groups of various kinds organized with an explicit Holiness doctrine.

Melvin E. Dieter provides an expert summary of these new denominations and the protests that led to them.[2] Dieter suggests that when the commitment of American Methodists to the new birth, to fervent holiness of life, and to the camp meeting began to waiver in the mid-19th Century, a series of protests arose. The Church of the Nazarene is one such church that arose as a result of these protests.

## THE HOLINESS REVIVAL IN AMERICAN METHODISM

Careful study suggests that the earliest Methodists in America gave an emphasis to Christian perfection similar to that among the Methodists in Britain. Methodism had found real destiny in America. Philip Schaff recognizes that

> "In America the Methodist Movement has had, perhaps, of all sections of the church, next to Puritanism, the greatest influence on the general religious life."[3]

---

[2] M.E. Dieter. <u>The Holiness Revival of the Nineteenth Century</u> Metuchen, N.J.: Scarecrow Press, 1980.

[3] Philip Schaff. <u>America: A Sketch of Its Political, Social and Religious Character.</u> New York: Charles Scribner, 1855, critical edition edited by Perry Miller (Cambridge: Harvard University Press, 1961, 137)

The Methodists were obviously growing. Donald Dayton points out that:

> "By the time of the American Revolution, Methodism in America was still an unorganized marginal sect with barely a foothold in the New World. But by 1820, the Methodists had grown abreast of the rapidly growing Baptists in membership and were well on their way to becoming the largest Protestant denomination in the United States in the 19th Century."[4]

Dayton further argued that by 1840 they had outnumbered the Baptists by a ratio of ten to six, and by:

> "a similar ratio of the combined membership of Presbyterian, Congregational, Episcopal, Lutheran and Reformed Churches."[5]

By the last half of the 19th Century, a spiritual malaise gripped Methodism. In spite of the favorable beginning, it is

---

[4]  Donald Dayton. <u>Theological Roots of Pentecostalism.</u> Metuchen, NJ: The Scarecrow Press, 1987, 63.

[5]  Hudson S. Winthrop. "The Methodist Age in America," <u>Methodist History 12</u> (April 1974) 11.

apparent that the doctrine of Holiness suffered a decline in the early years of the 19th Century. Many raised warnings of the neglect within Methodism of the doctrine of Holiness. William McDonald indicated that in 1824, the bishops of the Methodist Episcopal Church reminded the Church that the spread of Holiness was their purpose as a church and they warned against its being given up.[6]

In addition, it is believed that the reversal in the Methodist position on slavery six months after the 1784 Conference (this conference took a marked stand against the evils of slavery) also weakened the doctrine of Holiness in terms of its practical application. This was the practical issue that precipitated the withdrawal of the Wesleyans in 1843 and it had strong bearings on the beginnings of free Methodism in 1860.

Bishop Hamline in the introduction to George Peck's *The Scriptural Doctrine of Christian Perfection*, first published in 1841, stated that in his opinion, forty-nine fiftieths (meaning 98 percent) of the members of the Methodist Episcopal Church did not possess the experience of entire sanctification. Consequently, there grew a great interest in the subject. This great revival of Holiness was a marked feature of the middle

---

[6]   William McDonald. Double Cure p. 4.

and later years of the 19th Century. For the purpose of analysis, we could divide this revival into three periods:

I.   The early beginnings;

II.  The period of the great camp meetings;

III. The period of reaction.

It is important to note that revival had taken place prior to the mid-19th Century - the Second Great Awakening.

## THE SECOND GREAT AWAKENING

The Second Great Awakening began during the 1790's in New England with scattered renewals of piety in various towns. According to Sydney E. Ahlstrom it served to:

> "Transform the slumbering churches and make the 'evangelical united front' a potent force in the land"[7]

Revival came through camp meetings. The significance of these meetings was captured by Derek J. Tidball in *Who Are the Evangelicals?* As this passage notes:

> "From this awakening, camp meetings were bequeathed to future generations as a major

---

[7]   Sydney E. Ahlstrom. <u>A Religious History of the American People.</u> New Haven and London: Yale University Press, 1972, 7.

means of producing conversions, revivals, and holiness."[8]

In the Southern back country, Baptists and Methodists kept the first Awakening alive and carried it over the mountains to the new settlements in the Old Southwest. The most famous camp meeting took place at Cane Ridge, Kentucky. It was attended by up to 25,000 people from a mixture of denominations.[9] Sydney Ahlstrom argues that following this Second Great Awakening, revivalism became a steady feature of the Protestantism which emerged throughout the 19th Century and also into the 20th Century.[10]

The Great Revival altered the balance of churches in the South by augmenting Methodist, Baptist and Presbyterian churches where they had previously been weak.[11] Evidence suggests that these denominations appealed not only to whites but to many slaves who found, in the camp meetings, an emotional and expressive faith which helped them to both make sense of their present circumstances and to promise redemption in the world to come. This was a significant development, for the

---

[8]  Derek J. Tidball. <u>Who Are the Evangelicals? Tracing the Roots of Today's Movements.</u> London: Marshall Pickering, 1994, 57.

[9]  Ibid., pp. 57.

[10]  Ahlstrom, op.cit., pp. 387.

[11]  Tidball, op.cit., pg.57.

Methodists and Baptists were to play a similar role among the slaves in the Caribbean islands. In Jamaica, the Baptist missionaries had a strong appeal to the slaves.

During this early 19th Century period, the Shakers became a significant and influential source for those interested in communitarian experiments. The most distinctive feature of Shaker worship was the group dance. This dance, when accompanied by lively singing, could, at times, become quite frenzied. Ahlstrom contends that:

> "Shakerism was at once both an extraordinary embodiment of basic monastic motifs and a remarkable example of the special Christian emphases generated by revivalism."[12]

During the Second Awakening the Shakers' most successful camp was in Kentucky, when they carried off three former Presbyterians who had led the Cane Ridge revival, referred to earlier.[13] The Shaker communities became one of the American marvels and were visited by almost every systematic foreign observer, according to Ahlstrom.[14]

---

[12] Ahlstrom, op.cit; pp.494.

[13] Ibid. pp.493.

[14] Ibid. pp. 493-494.

The term "Shakers" has its West Indian equivalent. The Shakers found in Trinidad and Barbados are so-called because of their lively singing and characteristic frenzied dance in which their movements are described as "shaking." In Barbados, the group is also known as "the Spiritual Baptists" or "TieHeads." However, the group is a syncretistic mixture of African tribal and Christian religions, and in this sense differs markedly from the American Shakers.

The revival of the early 19th Century was described earlier as falling into three periods. During the early period, among the men who still testified to the experience of Holiness, was a Methodist minister by the name of Timothy Merritt. One of the first significant events that seem to point toward revival occurred at a camp meeting at Wellfleet, Massachusetts in 1819. Here Timothy Merritt preached on the baptism of the Holy Spirit, and as a result, a man named Wilbur Fisk was brought into the experience.[15] Both these men occupied important positions in the Methodist Church and they exercised their influence consistently for Holiness. In addition, two other events proved the real precipitation of the Holiness revival:

I. A revival at Oberlin College in Ohio under Asa Mahan and Charles G. Finney.

II. The Tuesday Meeting for the Promotion of Holiness.

---

[15]  Atwood. <u>The Abiding Comforter</u>, pp.97-102.

# THE OBERLIN MOVEMENT AND CHARLES G. FINNEY

**I.** The Oberlin revival brought a powerful visitation of the Spirit to Oberlin College. This spirit spread out across the country. It is impossible to discuss the Oberlin Movement and its impact without examination of the work of Charles G. Finney, one of America's foremost evangelists. Harvard Professor Perry Miller affirmed that "Finney led America out of the eighteenth century."[16] But who was Charles G. Finney?

Charles Grandison Finney (1792-1875) was born in Warren, Connecticut. He grew up in small towns of Oneida and Jefferson counties in Central New York. Finney returned to Warren for secondary schooling. In 1818, he began to practice law in Adams, New York. Here he came under the influence of a young Presbyterian minister, George W. Gale. Finney admired Gale personally, but disagreed violently with his theological views. Led by a personal reading of the Scriptures, Finney experienced a soul-shaking conversion in 1821. His career as an evangelist began the same week.[17] Many commentators have

---

[16] Comment take from Louis Gifford Parkhurst, Jr. <u>Principles of Sanctification: Charles G. Finney.</u> Minneapolis, Minnesota: Bethany House Publishers, 1986., 5.

[17] Ahlstrom. op.cit.; pp.458-461.

seen Finney as "the father of modern revivalism." In 1835, he accepted an appointment as professor of theology at Oberlin College. He served as president of Oberlin from 1851 to 1866. Sydney Ahlstrom argued that:

> "his dynamic presence made Oberlin a center of influence for revival theology, the 'new measures,' and a growing emphasis on perfectionism - all combined with an urgent sense of Christian activism."[18]

Commenting on the American revival of Christian perfection in the 19th Century, Donald Dayton had this to say:

> "The most influential of the Calvinist revivalist of the era came to be the controversial Charles Grandison Finney, advocate of a new style, 'New Measures' revivalism."[19]

Dayton argued that Finney's adoption of near-Wesleyan views on sanctification and the development of "Oberlin perfectionism" in the 1830s was the climax of this process of revivalism.[20]

---

[18]  Ibid. pp.461.

[19]  Donald Dayton. <u>Theological Roots of Pentecostalism.</u> Metuchen, NJ: The Scarecrow Press, 1987. 64.

[20]  Ibid. pp.64.

As a theologian, Finney is best known for his Revival Lectures and his Systematic Theology. Between 1841 and 1842, Finney published many sermons in the "Oberlin Evangelist." In these sermons he applied the doctrine of sanctification specifically to laymen.[21]

It is against this background that one can better understand the significance and impact of the Oberlin revival. Because the Oberlin movement significantly aroused a new interest in Christian perfection, some have thought that this was the key event that precipitated the revival.

**II.** The Tuesday Meeting for the Promotion of Holiness was launched by Mrs. Lankford in her home and later carried on by her sister Phoebe Palmer and her husband Dr. Walter Palmer. This, in 1835, may have had a more far-reaching effect in Methodism than the Oberlin revival. As such, I have chosen to mention it here. The meetings were first planned for ladies only, but were soon expanded for all. These continued until 1874. These meetings exerted a great influence inside Methodism. Many of the leaders became friends of the Palmers. The meetings also reached outside the Church and brought many individuals of different denominational backgrounds into a knowledge of

---

[21] Louis Gifford Parkhurst, Jr., <u>Principles of Sanctification</u>: <u>Charles G. Finney.</u> Minneapolis, Minnesota: Bethany House publishers, 1986. 9-13.

entire sanctification. This interdenominational "assimilation" as it can be called, was perhaps one of the greatest instruments of this period to help to bring about the revival.

The Holiness movement also made use of two traditional and still powerful evangelistic methods, that is, the use of literature and the staging of evangelistic meetings. As interest in the Holiness revival grew, Mrs. Palmer was active in writing on Holiness themes and her books received wide circulation. The Palmers also spread their work by evangelistic meetings. In 1839, Timothy Merritt launched his paper for the promotion of Holiness under the name of "The Guide to Christian Perfection."[22]

As a result of all this work, the doctrine of Holiness became well-known outside the Methodist Church. The Palmers were probably the best known advocates of Holiness in the years following the Civil War. Commenting on this period, Timothy L. Smith observed:

> "On the eve of the American Civil War, the stream of Holiness preaching in the United States approached its flood stage. A great revival swept the nation in 1858."[23]

---

[22]  Leslie Wilcox. <u>Be Ye Holy.</u> pp. 195-197.

[23]  Timothy L. Smith. <u>Called unto Holiness: The Story of the Nazarenes, the Formative Years.</u> Kansas City Missouri: Nazarene Publishing House, 1962. 11.

Just before and just after the Civil War, there were a number of outstanding Holiness books which no doubt played a significant missionary role. The period was also marked by a spontaneous outburst of daily prayer meetings and the development of Holiness camp meetings. Timothy Smith's account provides a vivid portrait of what took place:

> "Hundreds of mammoth daily prayer meetings broke out almost spontaneously in New York, Philadelphia,

Chicago, and nearly every city and town in the Northern states. Ministers and laymen of all denominations took part. Churches everywhere scheduled special services. A half million persons were converted."[24]

The period of the camp meetings began around 1865. Authorities seem to differ as to the date of the first suggestion. McDonald gives it as 1865.[25] The meeting was called the National Camp Meeting for the Promotion of Holiness. Out of that, a National Association was formed with the same name - The National Camp Meeting for the Promotion of Holiness. It therefore, moved from being just a meeting to becoming

---

[24] Ibid. pp. 11.

[25] William McDonald. The Double Cure. pp. 5.

an organization. The first camp was held at Vineland, NJ, July 17th, 1867. Leslie Wilcox notes that some of those involved were threatened with disciplinary action since this organization was seen as schismatic.26 The second camp meeting was held at Mannheim, Pennsylvania. It is believed that twenty-five thousand persons attended. The third year, the camp was held at Round Lake, New York. From 1870 onward, at least two camps, and sometimes several, were held each year.[27]

Because of the work of this national association, a great number of camp meetings and Holiness associations sprang up across America. Their impact was that of reviving the work of Holiness.

Despite these gains, there was a period of reaction to the revival. Some theologians and writers in the Methodist Church felt that it represented an extreme position.[28] The view was that with all the emphasis being placed on the instantaneous experience, the gradual phase was being overlooked. Many also arose to contend that sanctification was only gradual and there was no instantaneous experience to be looked for. This conflict was

---

[26]  Leslie Wilcox. Be Ye Holy. pp. 198-199.

[27]  Ibid. pp. 200.

[28]  Ibid. pp. 201.

counter-productive and had the effect of neglecting Holiness. Wilcox points out that "those within the Church feared schism and accused the holiness people of come-outism."[29] He also acknowledged that:

> "Most of the Holiness men had no intention of forming or advocating a separate ecclesiastical organization, and never did leave the parent church until circumstances seemed to make the continuance of their relation impossible if they were to continue preaching Holiness."[30]

To make matters worse, the rise within the Church of a liberal theology and the preaching of a social gospel made preaching of an experience of Holiness seem unnecessary and irrelevant. Commenting on the new responses to new challenges, Derek Tidball argued that:

> "Although social concern was originally closely connected with evangelicalism, the social gospel movement became more identified with liberalism."[31]

---

[29] Ibid. pp 202.

[30] Ibid. pp. 202.

[31] Derek J. Tidball, op.cit., pp. 63.

With the increased restrictions placed on these Holiness evangelists, splits seemed inevitable. For most of these men there was no alternative. Wilcox sums up this as follows:

> "The final step was taken in the limiting of the actions of these evangelists at the General Conference of 1894. Within a very few years, several new Holiness churches had come into existence."[32]

Why did the Holiness revival (movement) lead to the organization of independent churches, despite the frequent pledges of loyalty which its leaders made to the older denominations? Timothy Smith sought to address this question and offered the following four factors as influencing their decision to leave or stay.

I.  The persistent opposition of ecclesiastical officials to independent Holiness associations and publishing agencies;

II. The recurrent outbursts of fanaticism among persons who were members of the associations but not of the churches;

---

[32] Leslie Wilcox op.cit., pp. 203.

**III.** The outbreak in the 1890's of strenuous attacks upon the doctrine of sanctification itself; and

**IV.** The increasing activity of urban Holiness preachers in city mission and social work.[33]

The history of the Pilgrim (Wesleyan) Holiness Church, therefore, properly begins with the Holiness movement of the 19th Century.

---

[33] Timothy Smith. <u>Called Unto Holiness: The Story of the Nazarenes, the Formative Years.</u> Kansas City, Missouri; Nazarene Publishing House, 1962. 27.

# CHAPTER THREE

# THE HOLINESS MOVEMENT IN BRITAIN

Several books have been written on the life of John Wesley. What the literature seems to suggest is that throughout his life-time, Wesley maintained a personal loyalty to the Church of England. His desire was that his converts should remain within the Church. But the clergy of the Church and many of the leaders so opposed the Methodists that this became increasingly difficult. Wilcox has suggested that for most of his life Wesley insisted that the meetings of the Methodists should be conducted at a time that would not conflict with the services of the Church. However, the growing size of the work and the continuing outreach of the revival forced Wesley to take some steps which eventually led to separation.[34]

---

[34] Leslie Wilcox op.cit., pp.167-169.

In 1784, Wesley ordained Thomas Coke for the Superintendency of the American work. Dr. Coke has particular significance to the work of Methodist missions and mission strategy in the West Indies. He was the one who formally established a Methodist mission in Barbados in 1788. In addition to Thomas Coke, there were two other outstanding men among the Methodists in England in the early 19th Century. They were Adam Clarke, who once served as President of the Methodist Conference, and Richard Watson, who served as one of the General Secretaries for Wesleyan missions.[35]

Mention must be made of the impact of George Whitfield whose Calvinistic emphasis on predestination was opposed by Wesley and led to their growing apart, after serving together as itinerant preachers. The Welsh Calvinistic Methodists were formed as a result of the work of Whitfield.[36]

Careful review of the literature suggests that British Methodism was also influenced by American Methodism, and particularly by the visits of American evangelists in the 19th Century. There were periods of emotional fervor and rapid conversions. People were now learning that it was possible to "arrange" a revival. Charles Finney's "Lectures on the Revivals of Religion" became available

---

[35] Ibid. pp. 167-169.

[36] Ibid. pp. 169-172.

in Britain in 1839. These lectures taught that certain techniques could be adopted to encourage conversions.

Tidball wrote:

> "His writings led to fresh evangelistic activities and were reinforced by a visit of James Caughly, an American, to Methodist Churches in the 1840's."[37]

The 1858 Holiness revival in America had significant effects in Britain. There was an Ulster revival in Ireland in 1859 and a 'great awakening' in Scotland in 1859-60. A visit of Charles Finney gave impetus to this awakening. It was characterized by prayer, conviction of sin and many conversions. Leslie Wilcox is of the view that the first revival movement in England apparently was due to the evangelistic efforts of Dr. and Mrs. W.C. Palmer, mentioned earlier in this chapter. They began preaching in Northumberland in 1859 and visited other cities with great results. Historians and social scientists can often be at odds as to the significance of, and weight assigned to, particular historical forces in shaping the outcome of events. It seems to me that one thing is sure though; there was a distinct relationship between the growth of the Holiness movement in England and the rest of Great Britain and the visit of leading

---

[37]  Derek J. Tidball op.cit., pp. 45.

American evangelists. Other such evangelists included D.L. Moody and his singing colleague Ira D. Sankey. Moody made trips to England in a later phase of the revival from 1873-1875. Though he had an unpromising beginning, because of distrust of his revivalistic methods, he enjoyed major success in England and Scotland. In a four-month campaign in London, it is believed that he preached to more than two and a half million people.[38] During his visit at Cambridge University, there were also several conversions.

During the latter part of the 19th Century, preliminary conferences were held which finally developed into the "Keswick Movement." The Keswick teaching is sometimes thought of as being a different version of Holiness doctrine. It has a Calvinistic affinity and does not preach a true cleansing from sin, but only a power over sin. The Keswick Convention was first held in 1875 and became a key mark of the evangelical culture of the "leisured Christian classes."[39] It must also be recognized that Charles Finney and his colleague Asa Mahan played an important role in introducing interdenominational cooperation, and the acceptability of women's ministry. The focus placed on interdenominational cooperation was helpful in the creation of

---

[38] Ibid. pp. 45-46.

[39] Ibid. pp. 46.

the coming together of believers for Conventions. The Keswick convention is one such example.

As I conclude this chapter, I make a few observations about the English Holiness movement vis-à-vis the American Holiness movement. In the 19th Century, the English Methodists did not see the same quickening along Holiness lines that was evident in the American movement. Instead, English Methodists opposed revivalists' methods. The reality of this was evident in the exclusion of a native, William Booth. Booth was a Methodist New Connection Pastor who preached Holiness. It can be said that while the American Holiness movement saw great Holiness camps spring up all across the nation, the English Holiness movement saw the Keswick movement.

Finally, the great trend toward a social gospel and a liberal theology, which swept churches worldwide toward the end of the 19th Century, did, however, touch and leave its mark on the English Methodist groups. By the turn of the 20th Century, both the American and English Holiness movements shared this common feature.

The above survey does suggest that the Holiness Movement in the United States and Britain had, from the beginning, a strong missionary orientation. This orientation becomes evident in our next look at Missions to the Caribbean as we explore a link between Holiness and missions.

# CHAPTER FOUR

# THE HOLINESS MOVEMENT AND MISSIONS TO THE CARIBBEAN

In this chapter I examine the sources of the Holiness Movement in the English speaking Caribbean in general, and make some observations about the relationship of the Holiness movement to its parent churches in Barbados. I contend that the source of the Holiness Movement in the Caribbean was to be found in the diffusion of holiness ideas (teaching) through the establishment of "mission-type" churches. There is a strong relationship between Holiness and missions. In addition, one cannot comprehend the existing situation of the churches in the Caribbean without some understanding of the realities and nature of geography and history.

The chapter therefore begins with a discussion of the missionary bodies which were formed consequent upon the Holiness revival in America and England. It then reviews the missionary activity in the islands prior to the coming of Modern Holiness Churches. A few Holiness churches will be examined and discussed in the context of missions.

Given the historical relationship of the English Caribbean Islands to England and the geopolitical reality between the United States and the Caribbean islands, a number of questions emerge. One must bear in mind that during the 19th Century it was clear that an interest in the good government of the West Indian Islands was a big feature of the U.S.A.'s Caribbean policy. The geographical position of the United States has to a large extent shaped its political relations with the Caribbean islands. The avid student of history would agree that the United States' relationship with the Caribbean islands has been a mixture of realism and idealism. In this regard, a consideration of the geo-political context is helpful. Context provides a vantage point for us to better understand and examine something. These geopolitical realities are part of the context through which we must examine the nature of Christian mission activity in the Caribbean in this epoch.

Here are a few critical questions for consideration as we examine Christian missions to the Caribbean in this period:

1.  Did the Caribbean missions emerge out of the British or American Holiness Movement?

2. Were the Caribbean Islands considered a mission field?

3. Was the Holiness movement mission minded?

I posit these questions in order to stimulate some thinking on these issues.

Careful examination of the Holiness Movement in both Britain and the United States shows a strong relationship between Holiness and missions. In the 1800s in America, numerous societies for home and overseas missions were set up following the Second Great Awakening. These gave organizational shape to the Second Awakening and preserved its results in a way the first Awakening had failed to do. In general, revivalists seemed to have learned from their earlier experiences. Derek Tidball lists the following organizations and groups: An *American Board of Commissioners for Foreign Missions* established in 1810; *The New England Tract Society* (1814); *the American Bible Society* (1816); *The American Colonization Society for Liberated Slaves* (1817); *the American Sunday School Union* (1824); *the American Tract Society* (1825); *the Society for the Promotion of Temperance* (1826).[40] 1890-1914 became the age of missions. From a Caribbean perspective, one can agree with this assessment, for in this period a number of Holiness

---

[40] Derek J. Tidball. <u>Who Are the Evangelicals? Tracing the Roots of Today's Movements.</u> London: Marshall Pickering, 1994. 57.

churches were established. In this period, tremendous energy was poured into the Sunday School movement, Christian Endeavor, and reformed movements, such as the Temperance Movement. In 1886, the Chicago Evangelization Society was formed, later to become the Moody Bible Institute. The same year, the Student Volunteer Movement was formed. Its aim was the "Evangelization of the world in this generation."[41]

In England, the Cambridge Inter-Collegiate Christian Union became a significant group. It later became a symbol of evangelical orthodoxy in splitting from the Student Christian Movement in 1910. This was because the Student Christian Movement refused to make the penal view of the atonement central.[42] It must be pointed out that the SCM had grown out of the Student Volunteer Movement. The SCM subsequently became a non-evangelical student movement running in parallel with the Inter-Varsity Fellowship which was formed in 1927.

In his book, *A Religious History of the American People* Sydney Ahlstrom declared that:

> "One of the startling features of Professor Kenneth Scott Latourette's labors as a historian of the expansion of Christianity is his designation

---

[41]   Ibid. pp.63.

[42]   Ibid. pp.47.

of the nineteenth century, despite all its distractions and temptations, as 'the Great Century.'"[43]

This greatness he identifies as the evangelical enthusiasm that arose out of the Second Awakening. A new kind of religious institution emerged, the voluntary association of private individuals for missionary, reformatory or benevolent purposes. Similar voluntary associations were the feature in Great Britain in the 18th Century evangelical revival. Ahlstrom put missionary societies in perspective when he asserted:

> "no evangelical labor undertaken by the Churches
> had a larger rejuvenating effect than the foreign
> mission enterprise."[44]

The closing decades of the 19th Century witnessed the climactic phase of the foreign missions movement in the American Holiness Movement. This was due largely to the stimulus and inspiration of D.L. Moody. Many young people committed themselves to the cause of "the Evangelization of the World in this Generation."[45] The other essential contribution to mission

---

[43] Sydney E. Ahlstrom. <u>A Religious History of the American People.</u> New Haven and London: Yale University Press, 1972, 422.

[44] Ibid. pp. 424.

[45] Ibid. pp. 864.

activity was the work of the Young Men's Christian Association (YMCA). This organization also made significant advancement in American colleges and Universities in the latter decades of the 19th Century. Let us turn now to early missionary activity in the West Indies.

As suggested earlier, the spread of Christian missions in the West Indies has been conditioned by the political history of the region. The islands, which had been under the control of England, were influenced by Anglican and Protestant missionaries. By the end of the 18th century, Britain had occupied Barbados, Antigua, St. Kitts and Nevis, and Jamaica which was captured from Spain in 1655, Trinidad also from Spain, Grenada, St. Vincent, St. Lucia and Dominica from France. It should be noted that St. Vincent and Grenada, which were acquired earlier than others, are more "Anglicized." On the other hand, in Trinidad, Dominica and St. Lucia, because of the earlier Spanish and French presence, the Roman Catholic influence is strong (Spain and France were Roman Catholic nations).

Barbados can be described as one of the most English of the Caribbean islands. As a matter of fact, it was for a long time called "Little Britain" by its inhabitants. This is not surprising, for it was the undisputed British possession since 1627, never "changing hands" to any other European nation. Barbados is the only British Caribbean island never held by another Colonial power. As a consequence, ecclesiastically Barbados is very much an Anglican sphere, even today. The island is blanketed with parish churches and sub-parish churches. During the colonial period the work of evangelizing the slave was slow. During the 18th Century, it was left almost entirely up to the Anglican clergy, who were not as a rule conspicuous for missionary zeal.

An important date in the missionary history of Barbados is 1710, when by the will of Christopher Codrington, the Society for the Propagation of the Gospel (SPG) was enabled to establish a missionary training college for the West Indies (Codrington College). This was made possible by the bequest of two plantations, namely Society and Consett in St. John. Meanwhile, the society began a mission to the slaves in Barbados, and in 1712, they sent out Rev. Joseph Holt to perform "the ordinary duties of a missionary" and "to instruct in the Christian religion the negroes and their children within the Society's plantations in Barbados and to supervise the sick and maimed negroes and servants."[46] Another significant missionary milestone was the conservation of William Hart Coleridge as the first Bishop of Barbados in 1824. The seventeen years of his episcopate

------

[46] Charles H. Robinson. <u>History of Christian Missions</u>. New York: Charles Scribner's Sons, 1915. 396.

witnessed a great advance of missionary work among the slaves. Referring to the service which he conducted on the day of the emancipation of the slaves in Barbados (1838), he wrote:

> "It was my peculiar happiness on that memorable day to address a congregation of nearly 4,000 persons of whom more than 3,000 were negroes just emancipated. And such were the order, deep attention, and perfect silence, that you might have heard a pin drop. Among this mass were thousands of my African brethren joining with their European brothers in offering up their prayers and thanksgivings to the Father, Redeemer, and Sanctifier of all."[47]

Commenting on the work of the Society for the Propagation of the Gospel in Barbados and elsewhere in the West Indies, he added:

> "It was chiefly owing to the Society for the Propagation of the Gospel that that day not only passed in peace, but was distinguished for the proper feeling that prevailed and its perfect order."[48]

---

[47]  Ibid. pp. 397.

[48]  Ibid. pp. 397.

In my introduction, I made brief reference to the work of Protestant missionaries in Barbados, namely the Moravians and Methodists. The Moravians who began work in Barbados in 1765 developed significantly. They carried their work in the Dutch and Danish islands and for some time were strong in Antigua, Jamaica and St. Kitts. Missionary stations were also opened in Trinidad and in Tobago. The Wesleyan Methodists also did good work among the slaves. According to the census of 1901, the members of the different churches were as follows: Anglican 156,000; Wesleyans 14,400; Moravians 7,000; Roman Catholics 800; others 4,182.[49] From these figures it is clear that, apart from the Anglicans (understandably so) the British Methodists (Wesleyans) had a sizeable following. It should also be pointed out that the Roman Catholics were less visible than in other territories. This is not surprising given my earlier assertion about the relationship between political history and missions.

The Wesleyans and others who desired to share in the work of evangelizing the slaves were in many cases prevented from doing so by opposition from the planters. It should be noted that although the Methodists, Baptists and Moravians had come to the West Indies to minister to the slaves, they

---

[49]  Ibid. pp. 397.

had not come to attack slavery. Clement Gayle's analysis is instructive:

> "In his time John Wesley in his little book, *"Thoughts on Slavery,"* had attacked the white system of slavery and had warned Methodists against 'trading in human flesh,' but out of a practical consideration, that of having the opportunity of moving among the plantations, it seemed unwise at first to attack slavery."[50]

English Baptists began work in Jamaica in 1814 and continued to have good success. They also had missions in Trinidad, the Turk's Islands and the Bahamas. The Scotch United Presbyterians took over a mission in Jamaica in 1847 and also established a work in Trinidad.[51] From the foregoing it is clear that the Moravians, Methodists and Baptists were the most active Christian Missions operating in the West Indies in the 18th and early 19th century. In the latter 18th century, another group, the Evangelical Unity of the Brethren, set up a mission in Barbados in 1767. It was established "in order to

---

[50] Article entitled "The Church in the West Indies - Bondage and Freedom" by Clement. H.L. Gayle, 1980.

[51] Charles Robinson, op.cit., pp. 391.

bring salvation to the many thousands of Negroes on the island through a knowledge of Jesus Christ."[52]

During the late 19th and early 20th centuries, there was an influx of a "mission type" of church from America to Barbados. These Mission-directed churches (missionary controlled) were part of the driving force resulting from the Holiness Movement in the North. This influx also paralleled the development in other lands of the younger churches. Of significance, is the fact that the island of Barbados was undergoing rapid social change. The late 19th century and particularly early part of the 20th century was a time of social distress in the Caribbean. In Barbados, overpopulation, high unemployment, low wages, rigid stratification in terms of class and color, and poor living conditions led to social unrest in 1937. During this time of social unrest and social change, many turned to the New North American evangelical and Holiness churches, for they seem to appeal to the fervent religiosity of the Barbadian masses. These churches fulfilled their need for social acceptance and offered an alternative to the historic churches (Anglican, Catholic, Moravians, Methodist).

---

[52] Bossard Johann Jakob. History of the Mission of the Evangelical Brethren on the Caribbean Islands of St. Thomas, St. Croix and St. John Karoma Publishers, Inc. 1987, 5.

One such Holiness church was the Nazarene Church. The history of the Nazarene Church began with the Holiness Movement of the 19th century. The founding of the Church of the Nazarene is associated with Phineas F. Bresse, a former Methodist pastor.

Dr. Bresee had often said that the Church of the Nazarene was born in a Holiness revival.[53] This church is the largest of the Holiness denominations and has contributed the largest number of writers on Holiness. Its organization on a national basis took place at Pilot Point, Texas in 1908. Its membership at that time was drawn from associations of churches from cities and towns in the Northeastern, Western, Middle West and Southern States.[54] Hugh C. Benner in the preface to Timothy Smith's *Called Unto Holiness* argues that:

> "The driving force in the lives of early Nazarenes
> was a sense of mission, to the accomplishment
> of which they were utterly dedicated. This sense
> of mission was rooted in a vital experience of

---

[53] Timothy L. Smith, <u>Called Unto Holiness: The Story of the Nazarenes, the Formative Years.</u> Kansas City: Missouri: Nazarene Publishing House, 1962. 91-121.

[54] Ibid. pp.9-10.

scriptural Holiness and the implications of such
an experience in life."[55]

In a report to the General Assembly of 1905, Phineas
Bresee insisted that the primary task of the Nazarenes was "to
Christianize Christianity" and thus "to save America as a center
of religious life in the world."[56] The assembly agreed and urged
each congregation to begin at once giving a tithe of its total
income for foreign endeavors.

The Holiness Movement not only provided inspiration and
impetus for missions, but in terms of mission strategy, also
had practical models. The camp meeting was one such model.
Like the Methodists, the Nazarenes found that on most of their
mission fields, the camp meeting was an institution which was
easily adapted to evangelism in so-called agrarian societies.
Barbados seemed to have fallen into this "type" for in the writing of Timothy Smith on the formative years of the Nazarenes,
one finds a vivid reference to the experience of a missionary
Susan B. Fitkin in Barbados. He writes:

> "Susan B. Fitkin told of visiting a 'great people's
> meeting, out under the shining moon' on the

---

[55] Ibid. pp. 5 (preface)

[56] Ibid. pp. 251.

island of Barbados in 1928. Four hundred persons stood in an oval ring, singing and clapping, swaying to the rhythm of the music. The testimonies, the weeping, and the joy, she said, particularly when the group turned to singing songs about heaven, made her feel at home. 'It was a real American camp meeting off the little narrow Barbados street,' she wrote; 'at the close, three young men knelt and gave their hearts to God, adding the crowning touch of glory to that wonderful service.'"[57]

Smith argued that the informality of the atmosphere contributed to the development of native spiritual leaders (lay and ministerial). This vivid missionary story reflects two realities of Barbadian life: the hospitality for which Barbadian people are known and, the love for lively rhythms in the music (a general feature of Caribbean people).

The Methodists presence in the Caribbean islands developed in the late 18th Century. It should be pointed out that Methodism in the West Indies was originally connected both with Britain and the United States. In July 1791, the British Conference was held in Manchester, England. At this conference, it was reported that

---

[57] Ibid. pp. 346.

the increase for British Methodism during the year was 1,825 and that more than half of this gain was made in the West Indies and British America.[58] In *The History of American Methodism, Vol 1*, Methodism in the West Indies is described as beginning with the work of Nathaniel Gilbert, who preached to slaves. In 1778, John Baxter, a Methodist ship builder, is said to have left for Antigua to preach. Dr. Thomas Coke's Journal for June 2, 1785, notes that Baxter, along with Boyer, Turnell, Pigman and Foster, was ordained an elder at the conference which met at Baltimore June 1, 1785.[59] The history further points out:

> "Baxter's name appears in the Minutes for 1785 and 1786 as appointed to Antigua. In 1787, Antigua is no longer listed, and in 1788 Baxter's name is gone from the list of elders of the Methodist Episcopal Church."[60]

The 1791 Minutes show Samuel Rudder and Nathaniel Pinkard appointed to the West Indies. It seems that the American ties were growing weaker. These men from the British Methodists were not listed as elders of American Methodism.

---

[58] Bucke Emory Steven, ed. <u>The History of American Methodism Vol 1</u> New York Nashville: Abingdon Press, 1964, 417.

[59] Ibid. pp. 417.

[60] Ibid. pp. 417

After 1791, there is no mention of Antigua or the West Indies. However, the West Indian relationship with British Methodism now began to grow more firm. In 1792, Thomas Coke on his fifth voyage to America:

> "took Daniel Graham as the first missionary to the West Indies. Then, in 1799 the Wesleyan Conference 'resolved to take the West India Missions under its own care, recognizing Coke as its agent.'"[61]

Based on research elsewhere, this seems consistent with Coke's presence in Barbados at the time.

The Salvation Army's founder is associated with the name of William Booth. Mr. and Mrs. Booth were ardent advocates of Holiness. It can certainly be said, therefore, that the evangelical tenets of early Methodism were at the heart of its doctrinal statements. The Army first transplanted its work to America in 1880. In 1892, Barbados first attracted the attention of Salvationists when Major James Cooke, Adjutant Raglan Phillips and others visited the island on their way to Jamaica.[62] These men had come in search of three evangelists (Bayley,

---

[61] Ibid. pp. 417.

[62] Doreen Hobbs, Jewels of the Caribbean: The History of the Salvation Army in the Caribbean Territory. London: The Campfield Press, 1986. 56.

Plummer and Plum) who were said to be working on Army lines. Doreen Hobbs describes the occasion:

> "It was pouring with rain so they took shelter in a sugar warehouse and held their first meeting. Later, the Americans greeted them with warm hospitality before they went into the streets of Bridgetown, the capital. 'Oh, Salvation Army! Have you come to stay?' 'When are you coming?' The questions came thick and fast, so that before returning to the ship the group felt they must hold an open air meeting. The crowds amazed them"[63]

The relationship of the Holiness Movement in the United States to Barbados missions is clearly evident in the words appearing in "All the World" a few months following this meeting. It read:

> "Adjutant Phillips is looking with longing eyes on Barbados as a Salvation Army field. Certainly we seem to have pre-empted the island, since eight mission halls on Army lines are at work there, founded through the efforts of a Wesleyan

---

[63]  Ibid. pp.56.

minister who was blessed and baptized at our meetings in America."[64]

The Salvation Army in Barbados had come to stay. Since those early days, it had seen growth by the time Barbados gained its Independence in 1966. Hobbs describes that:

> "When General Frederick Coutts visited Bridgetown in 1966, he took the salute as 800 Barbadian salvationists marched past led by flags, bands and timbrelists."[65]

The Pilgrim Holiness Church is another example of the modern Holiness churches. Like the Church of the Nazarene, it was formed by a succession of unions between Holiness groups in various parts of the United States. According to Leslie Wilcox, the organization from which the denomination dates its origin was effected in the home of Martin Wells Knapp in Cincinnati in 1897.[66] Seth Cook Rees is seen as one of the founders of the Pilgrim Holiness Church. Rees was of Quaker extraction and during the Holiness camp meetings was known for his evangelistic efforts. According to Wilcox, the western conferences of

---

[64] Ibid. pp. 56.

[65] Ibid. pp. 65.

[66] Leslie Wilcox. <u>Be Ye Holy.</u> pp. 205-213.

the Holiness Church united with the Church and the name was changed to International Holiness Church. In 1922, two other bodies joined. One of these was the Pentecostal Rescue mission organized in 1897. The other was the Pilgrim Church. Seth Rees had been associated with the Church of the Nazarene but due to some conflicts, had organized the Pilgrim Church about 1915. After several unions, the name of the Church which had undergone several changes now became the Pilgrim Holiness Church.[67] The Pilgrim Holiness Church was another such church that entered Barbados as part of the "Holiness Mission" at the turn of the 20th Century. A discussion of the development of this church in Barbados is the focus of chapter seven.

The last two "Holiness Movement churches" that were transplanted in Barbados at the turn of the 20th century are: the Church of God (Anderson) and the Church of God (Cleveland, Tennessee). It is imperative here, that I give some attention to the use of the name "Church of God" since there are several denominations that share this title. They all share the common belief that there should be a return to the original New Testament Church. However, the doctrines of the various groups are not the same. Some denominations use this name without any added words except a parenthesis to indicate which group

---

[67] Ibid. pp. 237-238.

is under consideration (e.g. the above two groups). Others use the name "Church of God" with some added descriptive adjective or phrase. It should be noted that what is referred to as the "Church of God (Cleveland, Tennessee)" in the literature is now called the "New Testament Church of God" in Barbados and other Caribbean islands where it exists.[68]

The Church of God (Anderson) grew out of the revival work of John Winebrenner in Pennsylvania in 1825.[69] The birth of this church in the United States reflected the Holiness conflict over independent churches. According to the *Dictionary of Pentecostal and Charismatic Movements*, the emergence of this church was evidence of the vitality of issues other than Holiness teaching in the movement and to "the powerlessness of the Methodist Holiness evangelists to guide and control converts."[70] The Church of God (Cleveland, Tennessee) has

---

[68] In 1994, I discovered a church called "New Testament Church of God" on 63rd and Woodbine Ave., Philadelphia. U.S.A. After visiting and investigating this congregation I learnt that the Pastor, Rev. J. Barrett was a Jamaican. In addition, a large number of the membership were immigrants from the West Indies.

[69] Ibid. pp. 231.

[70] Stanley M. Burgess and Gary B. McGee, ed. <u>Dictionary of Pentecostal and Charismatic Movements</u> Grand Rapids, Michigan: Zonder van Publishing House, 1988.406.

been described as a classical Pentecostal denomination by the *Dictionary of Pentecostal and Charismatic Movements*. It is one of the oldest and largest Pentecostal bodies in America. The Caribbean islands were the first mission choice. This dictionary cites January 1910 as the time of the first Church of God missionaries going to a foreign country - the Bahamas islands.[71] It is not surprising then that the date for the establishment of the New Testament Church of God in Barbados is given as 1917.[72] A successful missionary ministry began in Jamaica in 1918.

In a report of a survey Commission authorized by the Inter- national Missionary Council issued by the Commission on World Mission and Evangelism of the World Council of Churches, the following evangelical churches, mission boards and organizations were said to be existing in Barbados. The survey was undertaken February - May 1961.

Barbados

1. American Baptist Home Mission Societies.
2. Anglican Church (The Church of the Province of the West Indies).
3. Christian Missions in Many Lands (Plymouth Brethren).

---

[71] Ibid. pp. 199.

[72] Date taken from the World Christian Encyclopedia David Barrett ed. Oxford, New York: Oxford University Press, 1982.

4. Church of God (Anderson, Indiana).

5. Church of God (Cleveland, Tennessee).

6. Church of the Nazarene.

7. Methodist Church (British).

8. The Methodist Church (U.S.A.).

9. Moravian Church.

10. Salvation Army

11. Pilgrim Holiness Church

12. Pentecostal Assemblies of the World.

13. Seventh Day Adventists

14. West Indies Mission

15. Worldwide Evangelization Crusade

16. Young Men's Christian Association (YMCA)

17. Young Women's Christian Association (YWCA)[73]

At the beginning of this chapter I posited a number of questions about missions and the Caribbean. From the historical data presented in this chapter, I believe it is reasonable to conclude that the Holiness Movement was very mission-minded. Following the establishment of independent Holiness churches, missions cause took on vigor. Many churches formed mission

---

[73] Table taken from the Report of the Commission edited by Wilfred Scopes and entitled <u>The Christian Ministry in Latin American and the Caribbean.</u> New York: World Council of Churches, 1962. 150.

boards. The Holiness Movement had certainly provided the impetus. The Caribbean islands were not to be left out as a mission field. It is also clear that the great majority of missions emerged out of the American Holiness Movement. This was obviously encouraged given the proximity of the Caribbean islands to the United States. The islands can be said to be lying in the "backyard" of America. There is a saying in the Caribbean that "if America sneezes, the Caribbean islands will catch a cold." This proverb, like many in the Caribbean, is rich in truth. American Holiness revivalism had certainly come to the Caribbean. While there is need for caution in terms of making generalizations, the reflection on missions to the Caribbean does point to the importance of geopolitical considerations in partly shaping mission strategy.

# CHAPTER FIVE

# THE WORK OF THE METHODIST MISSIONARY SOCIETY IN BARBADOS

Having surveyed the origins of the Holiness Movement in the United States and Britain and reflected on the relationship of the Holiness Movement to Holiness Churches in Barbados, this chapter focuses more specifically on the growth and development of the Wesleyan Holiness Church in Barbados and as such, is a case study exemplar of Christian Missions Strategy in the Caribbean. I present observations and draw some conclusions about missions and missions' strategy based on this "case study" approach.

The Wesleyan Holiness Church in Barbados is a product of the Holiness Movement in North America and its development reflected the same pattern of splits and mergers evident in the parent church in the United States. It grew out of a sense of mission and this sense of mission was rooted in a vital experience of Biblical holiness. It is apparent that the Wesleyan tradition was and is being perpetuated through the Wesleyan Holiness Church. Given the fact that the Wesleyan Holiness Church and the Methodist Church share the same ecclesiastical parentage which is traced to John Wesley, the Chapter begins with a brief review of the work of the Methodist Missionary Society in Barbados. By doing so, one is able to acknowledge the existence of a Wesleyan tradition in Barbados prior to the growth of the Wesleyan Holiness Church.

The history of the Methodist Missionary Society and the work of Methodist missionaries in the West Indies is a very interesting one. The Methodist Church was one of the first protestant churches to undertake foreign missions but one of the last to establish a Missionary Society. In this regard, one can speak of the work of Methodist missions on the one hand, and the work of the Methodist Missionary Society on the other. This historical distinction was well acknowledged by Noel Titus in his *The Development of Methodism in Barbados 1823 - 1883:*

> "The second reflection is that the missionary work in the West Indies was being adminis-tered by a Missionary Committee that was itself younger than he missions over which it presided.

While the Methodist missions in the West Indies formally started in 1786, it was not until 1813 that the Wesleyan Methodist Missionary Society was formed."[74]

History suggests that as early as 1760, Nathaniel Gilbert, a native of Antigua, who landed as proprietor and speaker of the House of Assembly, formed a Methodist Society of West Indian slaves. Gilbert is cited as the one who introduced Methodism in the West Indies. In this regard, the island of Antigua is seen as the early "launching pad." Nathaniel Gilbert visited England in 1758[75] and after hearing John Wesley preach, was converted to Methodism. On his return to Antigua, he sought to establish Methodism. Gilbert is therefore seen as the Father of Wesleyan Methodism in the West Indies. Gilbert died in 1774 and by that time, Methodism in Antigua had established itself among the blacks. It is clear then that Barbados was not the first island to have an organized group of Methodists. However, it was only some fourteen years later, during the first visit of Methodist Missionary Thomas Coke, that a Methodist mission was formally established in Barbados.

---

[74] Noel Titus, The Development of Methodism in Barbados 1823- 1883, Beine: Peter Lang Inc., European Academic Publishers, 1994.

[75] Findlay and Holdworth, Wesleyan Methodism, Missionary Society, Vol. II. 29.

Any account of Methodism in Barbados must therefore begin with the work of Thomas Coke. His work in missions was instrumental during the period prior to the establishment of the Methodist Missionary Society. Since he died in 1814, several months after the formation of the Methodist Missionary Society, his work must be seen in the context of the absence of any missionary society. He was greatly interested in missionary work and helped to send missionaries to West Africa for thirty years before the formation of a missionary society.[76] Thomas Coke visited Barbados on three occasions: in 1788, 1793 and 1805.[77] According to Francis Blackman:

> "His visit in 1788 resulted in the establishment of organized Methodism in Bridge Town which, within forty years, and in spite of its many vicissitudes, became the Wesleyan Methodist Church based in the city, ready for expansion throughout the island."[78]

---

[76] Charles H. Robinson, <u>History of Christian Missions</u>, New York: Charles Scribner's Sons, 1915. 479.

[77] Francis Blackman, <u>Methodism 200 years in Barbados,</u> Barbados: Caribbean Graphic Production Ltd, 1988. 1.

[78] Ibid., pp. 1-2.

On October 6, 1813, the Methodist Missionary Society was organized at Leeds, England. This society became responsible for missions overseas. With its formation, the supply of missionaries became more regular and financial support more constant in Barbados.[79] Commenting on the Methodist Missionary Society Noel Titus argues that:

> "The Methodist Society bore very largely the characteristics of a sect. It had been a movement of religious protest which had separated itself, or become separated, from the Church of England. Like any other sect, it showed all the vigor that is characteristic of a new movement. Its membership was by choice, since separation from an established body always involved risks, and continuance in membership was based on sustained evidence of commitment."[80]

It seems clear that there was a relationship between the Methodist Society in the West Indies and that in England. Changes in the West Indies were consequential upon changes in England. This was even more evident given the nature and

---

[79]   Ibid., pg. 22.

[80]   Noel Titus op.cit. pg.8.

force of the Anti-Slavery Society in England, and its impact on Caribbean Methodism and the slave system. Barbados was no exception. A few years following the establishment of a Methodist mission in Barbados (1788), the relationship between the Methodists and the Anglican (Established) Church turned sour. The opposition of members of the Anglican Church and of the plantocracy to the Methodists had its origin in the uncompromising stand which the Methodists in England had taken against slavery. Attitudes to Methodists which had developed in England were transported to Barbados and other West Indian islands. This was facilitated by the availability of information (letters, newspapers, magazines) from England to Barbadians. Blackman notes that:

> "In Barbados and elsewhere, the novelty of a new Christian teaching by a new branch of the Christian Church soon wore off and Methodism became suspect, especially since one of its basic principles was that all men, including slaves, were brothers in Christ."[81]

The attitude of the planters to the Methodist Missionary was one of decided opposition. The missionary was seen as a threat

---

[81] Francis Blackman, op.cit. pg.4.

to the well-being of the planters. To the Anglican clergy they were a thorn in the side. The fate of Rev. William Shrewsbury, a Methodist Missionary to Barbados is testimony to the vindictiveness and opposition of the planters and privileged groups in the Barbadian society. According to Blackman:

> "Shrewsbury was clearly uncompromising in his preaching of spiritual holiness and publicly condemning the evils of lying, concubinage, fornication, blasphemy, polygamy, and drunken-ness. These evils were mainly those of the white population, the free black and colored. On the other hand, the Negroes (slaves) were ill provided for spiritually in spite of a church (Anglican) being in each parish."[82]

Following Rev. Shrewsbury's preaching, there were several conversions. This led to resentment by the plantocracy. The threat posed by Methodism and by this preacher became very real. As a result on October 5th, 1823, Rev. Shrewsbury and his city chapel were attacked. The attack had received the support of the privileged members of the community and by October 20th, the building housing the residence and

---

[82] Ibid. pg. 25.

chapel were destroyed. On that same day Rev. Shrewsbury was forced to escape with exile from Barbados. The reports of the Shrewsbury case available to the Methodist Missionary Society were forwarded to the House of Commons in England. The House of Commons strongly condemned the slander of the Methodists and Shrewsbury was cleared of any blame. Blackman notes that:

> "The steps taken by the House of Commons thusextended to the colonies the Act of Toleration,which guaranteed freedom of worship and ofreligious assembly in England, and led to Buxton's statement that '...we will have religious toleration in the West Indies.'"[83]

Writing on this period, one of Noel Titus' major theses is that religious intolerance in the Barbadian society especially that linked to the existence of a church establishment was a major obstacle for the Methodists to overcome.[84] He further argues that the internal problems, regarding discipline in one congregation and class or color distinction among the ministers, created further difficulties for the Methodists.

---

[83]  Ibid., pg. 30.

[84]  Noel F. Titus op. cit.

It must be borne in mind that the establishment of Methodism in Barbados came against the background of the prejudices and tensions of a slave society. As a matter of fact, these prejudices did not end with slave emancipation. Titus contends that religious prejudice was still in evidence in 1883.[85] By the 1880s, Methodists were losing members; and, towards the end of the 19th Century, there were some concerns about Methodism. These concerns were about growing materialism and a desire for people to be more righteous.[86] This desire for people to be more righteous is a theme that re-emerges by the early 20th Century as the Pilgrim Holiness missions look at Barbados.

In the conclusion to his book, Noel Titus suggested that:

> "Methodists impact and influence were much broader than the actual statistics of membership imply."[87]

During my research in the Department of Archives in Barbados, I discovered a document written by Rev. F. Godson, a Methodist Minister, reflecting on his final years in Barbados (1913-20). In 1916, after two years in retirement, Rev. Godson

---

[85] Ibid.

[86] Based on a discussion and interview with Noel Titus, Anglican clergyman and Methodist Church Historian, Barbados, March 7th, 1996.

[87] Noel Titus op. cit. pg. 204.

was appointed for the second time to the Speightstown circuit of the Methodist Church after an interval of five years. He writes:

> "We found the circuit much changed and decayed. Death had been busy; migration to Bridgetown and overseas had taken serious toll; and competition by other denominations had increased and become much more aggressive. There was now quite a plethora of missions - Salvation Army, Christian Mission, with an offshoot, Seventh Day Adventists, etc. in addition to the Old Parish Church and ourselves - more than the population of a small place like Speightstown could possibly require or justify. However, we got to work and soon began to see encouraging signs.[88]

What Rev. Godson's reflection does suggest is that by the early 20th Century "a plethora" of holiness missions had emerged to pose a challenge to the Methodist Church in Barbados. While not specifically mentioned, it can be assumed that one of these missions was that of the Pilgrim Holiness Church. The early

---

[88] Rev. F. Godson, <u>A Half Century of Ups and Downs in the Eastern West Indies - Reminiscences of Rev. F. Godson</u> Methodist Minister Barbados: Chelsea Cottage, St. Michael, No. 17, 4th September 1951. 4.

beginnings of Pilgrim Holiness missions work there was conducted by a Brother and Sister Craig. They later secured a two-story building in Speightstown which led to the official opening of a mission there on February 4th, 1928.[89]

It is always instructive to observe how patterns tend to repeat themselves. Careful examination of the development of the Wesleyan Holiness Church in Barbados will show that, like its parent body in the United States in the late 19th Century, it was formed by a succession of splits, unions and mergers with various holiness groups existing in Barbados at the time. A brief synopsis of the Pilgrim Holiness Church in the United States is illustrative here. The Pilgrim Holiness Church in the United States was formed by the fusion of a number of Holiness Churches. In 1897, M.W. Knapp organized the International Apostolic Holiness Union in Cincinnati to encourage the preaching of primitive Wesleyanism. A series of mergers between various Holiness bodies developed, and in 1917, the name Pilgrim Holiness Church was adopted when the group was joined by former Nazarenes from the Pilgrim Church of California.[90]

---

[89]  Taken from a document entitled, <u>A Missionary's Cry From Island of Barbados, 1929-1930</u> by Wingrove Ives.

[90]  <u>Corpus Dictionary of Western Churches</u>, T.C. O'Brien (ed.) Washington, Cleveland: Corpus Publishers, 1970.599.

The discussion of the Wesleyan (Pilgrim) Holiness Church in this chapter is based on the compilation of facts from both written and oral sources.[91] In 1930, the Foreign Missionary Department of the Pilgrim Holiness Church sent out a little document in book form which described the work in Barbados. This document, entitled a *"Missionary Cry From Barbados,"* was the account and reflection of missionary R. Wingrove Ives. Its aim was to:

"Clearly set forth our grand objective in all our fields, with the prayer that God will use it to instruct, to encourage, and to stir the saints in the homeland."[92]

Rev. R. Wingrove Ives and wife, Mary C. Ives, came to Barbados on January 14th, 1919 and Rev. Ives was appointed District Superintendant of the churches a few months later.

---

[91] Written sources include, a missionary document; a report on church growth compiled for the Forty-third Annual District Conference, Barbados District; and the official Wesleyan Holiness magazine entitled "The Advocate." Vol.6, No.3. (May-June 1980). Oral sources included discussion and interviews with Rev. James Bend, a Wesleyan Holiness Pastor in Barbados. Rev. Bend has been involved in researching the churches' history in Barbados; discussion and interview with Rev. Carlisle Williams, Superintendent of the Barbados District of the Wesleyan Holiness Church; and several interviews with some older members of the Church in Barbados.

[92] Wingrove Ives, op.cit. Preface.

Rev. Ralph G. Finch the then District Superintendent, had appointed Missionary Ives in that capacity and he and his family returned to the United States.

The camp meeting in the United States, a vital feature of the Holiness Movement was no doubt "the breeding ground" for many missionaries. Rev. Ives' decision to come to Barbados was the result of a camp meeting in which he heard an address on missionary work in the West Indies given by Rev. Finch in 1917 in Milton, Pennsylvania. Rev. Ives notes that:

> "At which time we heard the call of God and offered ourselves for service in the regions beyond. It was not, however, until the following year, 1918, at the Beulah Park Camp Meeting, Pa., that we were asked by Rev. Geo. B. Kulp, who was then General Superintendent and also the Chairman of the Foreign Missionary Board, if we would accept a call to labor with Brother Finch in the West Indies."[93]

Rev. Ives had been Pastor at a church in Augustaville, PA. The Ives were really a missionary family - Rev. Ives was born in England, Mrs. Ives and first son John Wesley in Pennsylvania,

---

[93]  Ibid.pg.16.

U.S.A.; and, during their missionary work in Barbados, daughter Catherine Booth and son David Livingstone were born there. A striking observation is the naming of the children after ardent advocates of the Holiness Movement.[94] This missionary document is a major source of information on the early development of the Church since literary sources of information are either unavailable or lacking in detail. Rev. James Bend has suggested that the best living sources do not always agree on certain points. In addition, my thorough research at the Barbados Archives reveals information on the Methodist (Wesleyan) Church but nothing on the Wesleyan Holiness Church.

---

[94] John Wesley was the father of Methodism and Catherine Booth was the wife of William Booth, founder of the Salvation Army. Both were ardent advocates of holiness.

# CHAPTER SIX

# SOCIAL CONDITIONS
# IN BARBADOS

Any examination of mission strategy must take into account the nature of the "mission field" since missions often emerge out of the conditions of any epoch. We cannot separate the nature of mission activity from the lives of those who engage in those activities – the missionaries. Neither can we divorce mission activity and the missionary from normative history-graded influences. Normative history-graded Influences are those influences in the society that are part of that historical period of time. There is no doubt that people are influenced by the social and economic conditions of the time in which they live. In this regard, the perceptions of the missionary become significant. What then were the perceptions of the Pilgrim Holiness missionary about Barbados? Missionary Rev. R. Wingrove Ives described Barbados in the 1920s as suffering spiritually and socially. While all classes of people live in Barbados, he identified ninety percent as being poor. Low wages (20 cents to one dollar per day); unemployment, poor housing and disease were singled out for mention.[95] He writes:

> "To add to the distress, employment is often very slack. Thousands of the poor families live in dilapidated huts of only one or two rooms, and often amid very unsanitary surroundings; cone-candle sickness and disease are very common among them."[96]

Rev. Ives reflections were very graphic and he wrote rather assuredly about the conditions,

> "In respect to the social conditions, the people are not only immoral and poverty-stricken but they are also handicapped and debased by superstitions. One cannot talk with the West Indian natives, or visit their huts, or observe their habits without recognizing the fact that they are superstitious and that many of them still believe in 'obeah.'"[97]

---

[95] Ibid. pp. 9-10.

[96] Ibid. pg. 10.

[97] Ibid. pg. 11.

In this same vein he asserted:

> "The habit of drinking is another social evil that
> has a tremendous hold upon many of the natives.
> Surely it is a sad fact that in this, our little island
> home where poverty and want abound on every
> side, there are no fewer than 550 licensed liquor
> shops."[98]

This is a striking observation by Rev. Ives, for there is a saying in Barbados that "at every corner you will find a church and a rum shop." The "rum shop" has always played a significant role in the culture of Barbados. It is part of the rich cultural fabric. It is a place where people meet to do what Bajans call, "fire one" or "fire a few" which means to have one or a few drinks. However, it is not just a place to have a drink, but to discuss social issues and the "politics of the day." As a rich sugar colony, rum is a significant product of sugar cane and of the Barbadian economy. As it was in the 1920s when Rev. Ives made his observation, so it is today, rum continues to be an important foreign exchange earner for the island. According to the Barbados Private Sector Trade Team, between 2000 and 2014 Barbados maintained a positive trade surplus from rum

[98]  Ibid. pg. 11.

exports (Barbados' Rum Industry: An Analysis of the First Fourteen Years of the 21st Century,2014).

To my American readers, the "rum shop" is to Barbadians as the barber shop is to African Americans, particularly African American men. In the United States, the black barber shop has come to represent a place of significant activity. Outside of a haircut, it represents a safe place for social commentary about relationships, sports, politics, religion, economic issues, as well as a place for important male-bonding.

Rev. Ives quoted from an article printed in the Barbados Advocate (the local newspaper) at the time, as a way of attesting to the social conditions. The article, commenting on one city district, cited over-population, poor environmental conditions and illegitimacy as three evils that existed. The picture painted of Barbados by this missionary was one of "NEED":

> "BARBADOS IS IN NEED! The need is very great, the need is pitifully apparent, the need is a crying need; and there is only one answer to it. This answer is JESUS!"[99]

His observations and proclamations suggested a relationship between spirituality and social conditions and his Holiness

---

[99] Ibid. pg. 12.

emphasis is apparent. For these Pilgrim Holiness Missionaries, holiness was the theme for missions. The spiritual condition of Barbados was described as appalling:

> "While Barbados cannot be considered a raw missionary field, yet this island certainly is in need of Holiness missionaries - holy men and women with burdened hearts for the lost and with a vision of the opportunities and possibilities that are theirs to win others for Christ and to lead them into the light of full salvation."[100]

Rev. Ives recognized the presence and work of previous missions in Barbados but is unimpressed by their failure to bring Barbadians to a "life of Holiness."

> "And in spite of the noble work done by the early missionaries, namely, the Anglicans, Moravians, Quakers and Wesleyans, seventy-five percent of the births are illegitimate, and on every side sin abounds."[101]

---

[100] Ibid. pg. 9.

[101] Ibid. pg. 10.

Rev. Ives was deprecating to the Catholic Church and the white Catholic priests on the island, as well as other denominations and religious groups and expressions. In rather strong terms he claimed:

> "The spiritual conditions are appalling, for many so-called missionaries in this island are preaching anything but the Gospel of Jesus Christ; in fact, the Anglo-Catholic priests are leading thousands of people into Romish practices and superstition - Baptized Paganism. In some of the non-conformist churches that formerly stood for old-time religion, the Bible is being discredited, old beliefs are assigned to the melting pot, and the penitent form is entirely outlawed. There is plainly evident a mighty mobilization of evil forces against the truth of God, and on every hand there is seen an array of false cults."[102]

These cults are Theosophy, Christodelphianism, Spiritualism, Russellism, Christian Science, Bahaism and Seventh Day Adventism. Given this context, it is not surprising

---

[102] Ibid. pg. 9.

that there is a strong perception of Spiritual need, framed within a holiness theological context:

> "We feel there is the need of Evangelistic PilgrimHoliness missionaries to minister to the spiritualneed of the people of Barbados."[103]

Pilgrim Holiness missions in Barbados were therefore described as alive and aggressive, the missionary methods as apostolic and the objective as the salvation of lost and dying souls.[104] Missionary Ives's reflections strike in some places as somewhat paternalistic and ethnocentric;[105] however, his description of the socio-economic conditions adequately reflects the conditions of the early years of the 20th century in Barbados. It was these poor social and economic conditions that historians argue were the cause of the 1930s riots which swept Barbados and other islands that led to the formation of trade unions, political parties and the coming of social democracy.

---

[103] Ibid. pg. 9.

[104] Ibid. pg. 12.

[105] These are some of the descriptive terms used by Ives in reference to the people of Barbados and St. Lucia: "ignorant classes", "immoral", "it was quite difficult to keep order as the people were so degenerate," "poor native women," "poor unfortunate creatures," "baneful influence," "sin-cursed slum."

In addition, the Great Depression of 1929 in the United States helped further depress the economy. It is interesting that, even though writing in 1929, no mention of this is made in missionary Ives's correspondence. This omission and its associated failure to "connect the dots" of the geopolitical realities in the relationship between the United States and Barbados, and the Caribbean in general, is noteworthy. As the Depression deepened, a wave of mass strikes and violent demonstrations erupted across the Caribbean. In Barbados, several workers were arrested and imprisoned during the riots. These socio-economic conditions and the resulting social unrest seem to have created the right spiritual climate and sociological conditions for the acceptance of Holiness churches in the island. That all the members have a sense of participating in worship, that these churches became a focal point for warm social life where people seemed important and cared for each other became a powerful attraction. It is against this background that the Pilgrim (Wesleyan) Holiness Church developed in Barbados.

# CHAPTER SEVEN

# THE GROWTH OF THE WESLEYAN HOLINESS CHURCH

The Wesleyan Holiness Church has a rich and exciting history. Rooted and grounded in the teaching of John Wesley, the church embraces the **spreading of scriptural holiness. As** discussed earlier, **the growth of the Wesleyan Holiness Church in the Caribbean is linked to** events in American Christianity.

## EARLY BEGINNINGS

The original Pilgrim Holiness Church existed as an interdenominational work.[106] This is not surprising, given the various mergers that gave rise to its formation. It was out of this interdenominational body that the missionaries were sent to

---

[106] Ibid. pg. 13.

the West Indies. One such organization was the International Holiness Union and Prayer League.[107] In describing this period Ives notes:

> "The most outstanding of these soldiers of the Cross was Rev. C.O. Moulton whose ministry was mightily owned and blessed by God, especially in the island of Barbados. Later, Rev. James M. Taylor visited this island with an evangelistic party, and many were reached with the message of salvation and sanctification."[108]

Moulton's missionary work involved several islands. James Bend believes that he began his work in St. Kitts early in 1902[109] and that he died in British Guiana (Guyana) in 1909. The date of his death seems relatively accurate, since by the permanent organization of the Pilgrim Holiness Church in 1912, he was no longer on the scene and his death had been lamented. Oral evidence suggests the years 1901-1907 as the time of his missions

---

[107] Taken from the "Report on Church Growth" presented at the Forty-third annual District Conference of the Wesleyan Holiness Church, Barbados District.

[108] Wingrove Ives op.cit. pg. 13.

[109] Discussion with Rev. James Bend March 9th 1996 (Barbados)

in Barbados. In an assessment of his work, James Bend had this to say:

> "His ministry was blessed, and many persons were saved. His ministry was not without its difficulties for he labored during a time when there was some disquiet as to the conduct of some missionaries. Attention had been drawn around this time, to a couple of missionaries called Brother Penny and Sister I.D. Haines around whom there was much controversy, arising out of their financial practices in relation to their followers."[110]

It is believed that similar difficulties forced Moulton to leave Barbados for British Guiana. Following Moulton's death, Rev. James M. Taylor, mentioned in missionary Ives's account, came to Barbados in 1909 and pioneered a number of successful evangelistic campaigns. The consequence of this work was the formation of "Faith and Love Mission" - a mixture of former Moulton followers and converts from the Taylor services. James Bend explained that:

> "The Rev. Taylor offered leadership for only a short time. He returned to America about late 1909 or

---

[110] Forty-third Annual District Conference, Report on Church Growth, Barbados District. Written by James Bend.Pg.1.

early 1910. The members of the newly organized Faith and Love Mission were again left leaderless. They were also homeless. They had services at the Salvation Army Hall, and sometimes at the Y.M.C.A. Because there was no leader or fixed meeting place, a falling away of members took place. The faithful few preserved, and soon they were able to rent a meeting place at one dollar a month."[111]

Two things seem evident from this early beginning:

(1) There was a great degree of cooperation between various holiness groups;
(2) There seemed to be a focus on the city of Bridgetown (the capital) as part of the mission strategy.

The use of the Salvation Army Hall is evidence of such cooperation, the Salvation Army itself developing out of the Holiness Movement. One must remember that as early as 1892, the Salvation Army had looked to Barbados as a mission field and had identified eight mission halls on Army lines at work in Barbados, founded through the efforts of a Wesleyan minister. By May 1898, the Army had set up temporary quarters in Nelson Street (City of Bridgetown). Plans were also made to

---

[111] Ibid. pg. 2.

make Barbados the divisional headquarters of the Army in the West Indies, with the intention of establishing stations in each of the neighboring islands.[112]

## THE FIRST MISSION HALL

The first Pilgrim Holiness mission hall in Barbados was a rental hall situated at the corner of Swan and Lucas Streets in the city of Bridgetown. It was known as the "Outlet Hall." Missionary Ives described this landmark accomplishment as follows:

> "located in an upstairs room, fifteen by forty (above a rum-shop) with a low ceiling and with very poor ventilation, the Gospel seed was sown and watered by the tears and the prayers of our first humble missionaries and faithful people."[113]

James Bend wrote:

> "Here our ancestors settled; here they met; here they prayed; here they preached the Gospel of Jesus Christ."[114]

---

[112] Doreen Hobbs, <u>Jewels of the Caribbean: The History of the Salvation Army in the Caribbean Territory</u> St. Albans: The Campfield Press, 1986. 57.

[113] Ives op.cit. pp. 13-14.

[114] James Bend op.cit. pg. 2.

In 1912 Rev. James Taylor returned to Barbados and to the "Faith and Love Mission". He was accompanied by Rev. R. G. Finch, Rev. Reinbarger and Rev. Decamp. This group re-organized the mission to reflect the name of the parent Interdenominational body in the United States. The new mission was now called the "Apostolic Holiness Church". James Bend wrote:

> "The Rev. Taylor moved on, leaving the work under the supervision of the Rev. Finch who is usually credited with having first organized the church in Barbados. The Rev. Finch did not remain long with the church. He returned to the United States the very year. Once again the luckless band was left leaderless."[115]

Leadership is always a crucial aspect of missions. The success of missions' efforts is tied to the availability of competent leaders. Here it was of no less significance.

> "How they survived during the years of apparent neglect is not known. Obviously there would have been some person or persons who assumed local leadership of the group and helped to carry

---

[115] Ibid. pg. 3.

on in the absence of missionary leaders. It seems as if only missionary leadership was recognized, and that local leadership, which obviously there had to be, was disregarded - at least as far as recording and giving credit were concerned."[116]

Bend's insightful question and response points to an interesting concern of mission strategy in the Caribbean. This is the extent to which mission-directed churches (missionary controlled) favor or foster the development of native spiritual leaders. The preceding research suggests that the early development of the Wesleyan (Pilgrim) Holiness Church was a mixture of two models of churches. Firstly, a Mission-directed church (missionary controlled); and a National front church where national leadership was working with but usually under the direction of missionaries.

In 1916, Brothers James D. Tucker and Missionary George Beirnes came from British Guiana to Pastor the work in Bridgetown. One year later (1917), the Whitepark Tabernacle, St. Michael, was constructed. This first locally-owned church replaced the old mission hall as the place of worship. The acquisition of any physical structure during the establishment

---

[116] Ibid. pg. 3.

of missions is always a remarkable achievement. This was very evident, for in the words of Ives:

> "It was not only a memorable day in the history of the church in Barbados when it was completed and dedicated to the Lord by Brothers Beirnes and Slater, but it was also a day of great joy to all the Pilgrims."[117]

The date of 1917 has been used in the past by early Barbadian Pilgrims as the beginning of the church in Barbados. However, the preceding research suggests that there was much mission activity prior to this date. The date 1917 seems to have been used because it was the date of the acquisition and erection of the first building of Whitepark, St. Michael.

Bend has suggested two periods in the church's history:

(1) 1912-1917 (early beginnings)
(2) 1917-1980 (growth and development)[118]

Based on the evidence, one must also add the period 1908-1910 as part of the early work. The year 1912 is a significant year in the history of the church, for according to the Official

---

[117] Ives op.cit. pg. 14.

[118] Discussion with James Bend, March 9th 1996 (Barbados)

Registry of the Barbados Government, "Outlet Hall" was first established and registered by George Beirnes as a charitable Christian Organization.

## SPLITS, MERGERS AND EXPANSIONS

In the period following the establishment of the Whitepark Church, there was an expansion in the Pilgrim Holiness Church in Barbados. Several outstations, which were formerly independent missions, were taken over by the church. The strategy of missions evolved as follows: from street preaching, open air meetings, and cottage meetings to the establishment of "Outlet Hall" in the city. The establishment of missions in various parishes followed. The concept of "mission hall" is evident in the early work; some of these were rented halls. The worship patterns and mission strategies, which were developed in Holiness camp and cottage meetings in the United States, were transplanted either through adoption or adaptation to the Pilgrim Holiness church missions in Barbados. The mission hall and tent meeting were two such strategies. Tent meeting was a significant strategy in the development of the Kew Land ("Mount of Praise") Church. In 1925, the mission in Barbados was given a Gospel tent by the Circleville, Ohio, Camp meeting.[119] This

---

[119] Ives. op.cit. pg. 25.

tent, erected on the spot of land owned by the church, became the focus of an intense evangelistic campaign for one month. Missionary Ives described the results as splendid. In this case he wrote:

> "At the close of the tent meeting a temporary hall was rented in which to carry on the work, and the church and Sunday School reorganized. The new work started in a revival atmosphere with the former members and a splendid band of new converts, and with constant additions it was not long until the place became too straight to hold the crowds."[120]

The Immanuel Mission had sought to establish a church building on this spot prior to 1923. However, a lack of funds hampered that establishment. On this occasion, the Pilgrim Holiness Church, assured of financial assistance from the "Church of Christ in Christian Union", Ohio, U.S.A., began construction of a building. Ives noted that:

> "In less than three months after its completion very bill was paid."[121]

---

[120] Ibid. pg. 26.

[121] Ibid. pg. 28.

The Church was opened October 3, 1927 and was pastored by Rev. and Mrs. J.A. Boyce. Missionary Ives writing in 1929, described the Kew Land Church as having the second largest membership (over 150 members) in the Pilgrim work in Barbados.

From the formation of mission stations in several parishes, the next phase of the mission strategy saw the establishment of church buildings, many of which were a result of mergers with other holiness groups. In 1923, ten churches of the Immanuel Mission merged with the Pilgrim Holiness Church. The church's property, membership and scope were significantly increased as a result of this merger. Based on the data, it is clear that Church merger was an important feature of early mission strategy in Barbados, a feature that facilitated the survival of individual churches.

Another significant pattern was the pioneering of branch missions by individual churches in nearby communities. The New Orleans Mission and Black Rock Mission are two cases in point. These were pioneered by the Whitepark Church and Kew Land Church respectively. Of the New Orleans Missions Missionary Ives in 1929 wrote:

> "A number of souls were saved here in the open-
> air meetings conducted by the Whitepark Open-

Air Bands, and the Lord has also been pleased to give us seekers in the new mission. New Orleans is certainly a real missionary district."[122]

James Bend commented that:

"Wherever its members went, they preached the three-fold message of salvation from sin, the sanctification of believers, and the living of a sober life. This three-fold message became the distinctive mark of the Pilgrim Holiness Church."[123]

The Black Rock Mission was opened by Pastor J. H. Boyce and Rev. Ives.

These cases are excellent examples of the kind of cooperation and commitment that existed among local believers. In terms of financial support, it is clear that this was provided by Holiness Churches and missions in the United States; however, the importance of local support was evident. Large portions of the cost of many churches were paid by local funds. A large majority of these mission stations, mentioned in this chapter, have become the permanent homes of Wesleyan (Pilgrim) Holiness Churches today. By 1929, there were twenty-nine

---

[122] Ibid. pg. 25.

[123] Bend op.cit. pg. 4.

mission stations with a membership of 1,288 and a Sunday School enrollment of over 2,500[124] (see Appendix I). Missionary Ives described this success as a monument to the self-sacrifice of the Holiness people in the homeland (U.S.A.) as well as in Barbados.[125]

One unique feature of the early missions in Barbados was the establishment of mission stations at the Leper Asylum and the Almshouse, both situated in the parish of St. Michael. Ives described what is an impressive story behind the creation of the Leper Asylum Mission:

> "In the months of February, 1918, Sister Mary Hinds, one of our faithful Whitepark members, was pronounced a leper and was taken to the Lazaretto. This precious saint of God took this terrible ordeal in the spirit of a true soldier of Jesus Christ, and set about to make the best of her lot. Seeing an open door for service for her Master she started a Holiness Sunday School in May 1918, with an enrollment of thirty."[126]

---

[124] Ives op.cit. pp. 16-17.

[125] Ibid. pg. 17.

[126] Ibid. pg. 33.

Sister Hinds was assisted by two "Bible women" from the Whitepark Church, Sister Rock and Sister Pickett. The Mission at the Almshouse was organized by Rev. R.G. Finch and Rev. Ives in 1920. A sister Florence Clark of the Carrington Village Church is credited for its continued work.

## OTHER INDIVIDUAL CHURCHES

The Carrington Village Church in St. Michael was organized in 1918. In the late 1920s, it was pastored by Rev. J. D. Tucker and Sister Philomena Dummett was the assistant pastor. It is believed that both of these were converts of the Church in British Guiana. Besides the regular services, the Church had developed other significant ministries. These included a weekly Young People's Bible Class, a Women's Meeting, a Vocal Music Class, and a Teacher's Training Class. Rev. Ives described it as one of the best systematized churches in the organization, being both spiritual and aggressive.[127]

The Dean's Village Church was dedicated June 10, 1928. This church was also pastored by Rev. J. D. Tucker, and during its early formation held services under a tent. These two churches were also recipients of financial support from

---

[127] Ibid. pg. 29.

Holiness groups in the United States. One third of the building cost of the Carrington Village Church was given by the Church at Battle Creek, Michigan. The Dean's Village donor was the Dove Band in Columbus, Ohio. The money was given as a memorial to their founder Aunt Mary Wright.[128] In 1931, oral reports suggest that there were some difficulties between Rev. Tucker (Pastor) and the Dean's Village and Carrington's Village churches. These difficulties resulted in the first split in the Pilgrim Holiness Church. The Dean's Village Church left the organization and formed the Tucker Memorial Church. In the absence of any clear evidence of the cause of this split, some critical questions emerge:

1. What could divide members of the Holiness movement?
2. What are the theological and Biblical implications of traditional holiness themes?

It seems to me that splits were inevitable, for doctrinal and theological controversies often accompanied the teaching of Holiness among Barbadian Pilgrims. History has a strange way of repeating itself. One must also bear in mind that restrictions placed on holiness believers (like those in the U.S.A. in the 19th Century) were often controversial.

---

[128] Ibid. pg. 31.

The same Holiness themes that brought holiness believers together in unions and mergers had the seeds to also divide them. Additionally, in explaining church splits, one must not overlook the role played by such factors as individualism, conflicts over leadership style, personality conflicts and ego-oriented behavior. These factors are all evident in the history of Christian Missions.

The 1920s was a period of rapid expansion, both in terms of church membership and church property. This expansionism was a result of a merger, and the evangelistic and pioneering efforts of local believers. The amalgamation of the Immanuel Mission in 1923 brought the following missions:

> Fustic Village, Crab Hill and Pie Corner in St. Lucy; Church Village and Ragged Point in St. Philip; Lodge Road in Christ Church; Dean's Village in St. Michael; and Ellerton and Wobourne in St. George.

Six Roads and Martin's Bay churches were organized in 1920; Massiah Street in October 1921, followed by the churches at Edgecliffe and Welch Village, all in the parish of St. John. The Church of Maxwell around 1924; Sargeant Village and Hothersal Turning in 1927 and Speightstown, St. Peter in February 1928. By 1929, there were no mission stations in only two of the eleven parishes - St. James and St. Andrew. In Proute, St. Thomas and Bragg's Hill, St. Joseph, there were rented halls.

Two things are repeatedly emphasized in the report of missionary Wingrove Ives:

(1) The faithfulness and loyalty of local workers in terms of evangelism and discipleship, and in terms of payment for the construction of local buildings.
(2) The message of scriptural holiness and free salvation.

## FROM PILGRIM HOLINESS TO WESLEYAN HOLINESS CHURCH

One of the most significant mergers in the history of the Pilgrim Holiness Church came in June 1968 when the Wesleyan Methodist Church merged with the Pilgrim Holiness Church. With this merger, the denomination became the Wesleyan Church. Given the fact that the Pilgrim Holiness Church was close in doctrine and polity to Methodism, and in agreement with Wesleyan doctrines, there was no shift or change in doctrinal emphasis when the two churches joined. The Wesleyan Methodist Church adheres to Wesleyan doctrines and stresses holiness. In Barbados and other Caribbean islands, the church became the Wesleyan Holiness Church.

This merger led to some uncertainty among Barbadian adherents. It reflects the tension between the "Old" and the "New." Many elderly believers tended to see themselves as "Pilgrims" whereas the younger believers, particularly those coming into the church after 1968, have no strong allegiance to the "Pilgrim Tradition." To make matters worse, many churches did not change the name of the church engraved on their front walls. They still carried the title "Pilgrim Holiness Church." Ecclesiastically, the organization was the "Wesleyan Holiness Church" but legally it was the "Pilgrim Holiness Church" since this is what is inscribed in the Articles of Incorporation in Barbados. Local church administrators in Barbados had not made this legal adjustment. James Bend was of the view that the Pilgrim Holiness Church was more mission-oriented, more vibrant in missions, whereas the Wesleyan Methodist Church brought a more established, organized machinery.[129]

Today the Wesleyan Holiness Church in Barbados continues to have a holiness focus and link with its Methodist (Wesleyan) tradition. Here is an example of a unique way in which this can be seen. A few pastors in the Barbados District attended Asbury Theological Seminary in Wilmore,

---

[129] Discussion with Rev. James Bend, March 9th 1996 (Barbados)

Kentucky to pursue graduate studies. This was facilitated by the fact that this Seminary readily accepted academic credits from the Caribbean Wesleyan College in Barbados (now defunct), where these ministers had done their theological training. The story of the history and tradition of Asbury Seminary is of some interest here. In 1890, John Wesley Hughes, a member of the Methodist Episcopal Church South, organized Asbury College. In 1923, the President of Asbury, Henry Clay Morrison, founded Asbury Seminary as a part of Asbury College.[130] Later it was made a separate institution and eventually occupied its own campus adjacent to the college. Today the seminary foundation of the Wesleyan Church is associated with Asbury Seminary in Wilmore, Kentucky.[131]

As I conclude this chapter, I wish to make some further observations about the work of the Pilgrim Holiness missions to Barbados. The research suggests that Barbados was used as a "launching pad" for further missions to neighboring islands, namely St. Lucia and St. Vincent. Like Barbados, these islands were seen as "needy fields." Around 1919-1920, Rev. Wingroves

---

[130] Leslie Wilcox, <u>Be Ye Holy</u> pp. 222-223.

[131] Frank S. Mead, <u>Handbook of Denominations in the United States (6th Edition)</u> Nashville, New York: Abingdon Press, 1975. 273

Ives and others first visited St. Lucia and suggested that there was a need of a Full Salvation Mission work there. In March 1923, they revisited the island with General Foreign Missionary Superintendent, Rev. R.G. Finch, and Rev. Charles Slater.[132] Rev. Ives later wrote:

> "On our return to Barbados the matter was thoroughly talked over and arrangements made forthwith to send Rev. and Mrs. C.P. Jorge, two of our workers in the Barbados District, to St. Lucia to open up a work in this sadly neglected field. These workers, converts of our church in British Guiana, S.A., arrived in St. Lucia, April 12, 1923, and succeeded in renting a hall where a series of revival services was commenced within three days."[133]

Missionary Ives emphasis on Holiness and full salvation continued. Given the strong influence of Roman Catholicism in St. Lucia (98%), establishing a Pilgrim Holiness Church there was a discouraging task. Rev. Ives believed that as Holiness missionaries, they had the "real" message and his journal reflects

---

[132] Ives op.cit. pg. 60-62.

[133] Ibid. pp. 60-63.

a very negative attitude towards Adventists and the established churches - Anglican and Roman Catholic. While describing a scene of Roman Catholics kneeling at a cross in St. Lucia on Good Friday, 1927, Rev. Ives charged:

> "Rome has plenty of crosses for her followers, but no Christ to save, sanctify and keep from sin."[134]

His dogmatic views were clearly evident:

> "How different it might have all been if the people of the Protestant denominations had really had the vision of a lost world and had been as anxious to spread full salvation as the Papists have been to ensnare the people of these West Indian islands with the dogmas of Rome."[135]

He described the Roman Catholic practices as idolatrous worship and the moral conditions in St. Lucia as very bad. In his opinion, "There is not a more needy place for Full Gospel Missionary Work in the West Indies than St. Lucia."[136]

---

[134] Ibid. pg.64.

[135] Ibid. pg. 65.

[136] Ibid. pg. 64.

Rev. Ives's theological perspective and perception of need were no less evident in St. Vincent:

> "When we visited it in May, 1927, we were favorably impressed with the place, and we believe a good work could be done if a fire-baptized Holiness preacher could be sent to open up a mission; but we have not as yet been able to send a missionary to this sadly neglected field."[137]

## THE ROLE OF WOMEN IN MISSIONS

My second observation relates to the role of women in missions. The data presented in this chapter suggests that women played an important role in the growth of Pilgrim Holiness missions in Barbados. In 1929, the Barbados District was described as having one ordained deaconess and three Bible women. Several local women played leadership roles as assistant pastors (in some cases with their husbands), and in cottage meetings, prayer meetings, open-air meetings, Sunday School, Women's Meeting and missions work in the Almshouse and Leper Asylum. The Church documents and reports are replete with the names of several faithful women who became a major part

---

[137] Ibid. pg. 66.

of the foundation of the Pilgrim (Wesleyan) Holiness Church in Barbados. The names of Sisters Philomena Dummett, Mary Hinds, Florence Clark, J.A. Boyce, Ince, Rock, Pickett, Graham, N.C. Ecklund, Harewood, J. W. Humphrey, and Craig ring loud. These cases are testimony to the significant role played by women in the development of the Caribbean Church. This is a pattern that must be acknowledged in Caribbean church history and missiology since it has received little attention.[138]

## A WORKING CLASS FOCUS

Thirdly, the Wesleyan (Pilgrim) Holiness Church in its development was certainly a lower class (grassroots) church. It catered to many working class families. On several occasions, whole families were converted together. The Carrington Village Church in St. Michael had a ministry that sought to cater to the

---

[138] Women's leadership in the Holiness Movement and the Movement's support for women's ordination has received extensive documentation in works such as Nancy Hardesty's <u>Women Called to Witness: Evangelical Feminism in the Nineteenth Century</u>, Nashville: Abingdon Press, 1984. The pioneer essay is Lucille Sider Dayton and Donald Dayton, "Your Daughters Shall Prophesy: Feminism in the Holiness Movement," <u>Methodist History 14</u> (1976):67-92.An in-depth documentation on women's leadership and contribution to the development of Holiness Churches in Barbados would be a great contribution to Caribbean Historiography.

material needs of members. They aided members in time of sickness, maintained a fund for them in time of death and assisted those who needed clothing in order to come to church and Sunday school. Missionary correspondence showed appeals to supporters in the United States for clothing and good literature for Barbadian believers. There is a sense in which the development of the Pilgrim (Wesleyan) Holiness Church was part of the grass roots' struggle to make sense of its social existence in early 20th Century Barbadian society.

Finally, despite the merger with the Wesleyan Methodist Church in 1968, the Church in Barbados retained something of its own identity. While the Church in the U.S. is called "The Wesleyan Church," that in the Caribbean is called "The Wesleyan Holiness Church." This, together with the example of the New Testament Church of God referred to in chapter four, reflects the fact that while West Indian Holiness Churches emerged out of the holiness revival in the United States, they maintained their distinctive Caribbean flavor. In the early and mid-twentieth century, the Caribbean Church was, and continues to be **a Kindle in the Kingdom.**

The Wesleyan Holiness Church in Barbados must be understood as having historical and theological roots in Methodism and ties to the broader Holiness Movement. This reality reflects a significant relationship between spiritual renewal and missions – an essential thesis of this book. **There is a "kindling" that happens, an igniting and inspiring that we might call spiritual renewal.** **This** spiritual awakening or renewal is often the basis for missions, for when the fire of spiritual renewal burns in our hearts we tend to be drawn to the great commission – *"¹⁹ Therefore go and make disciples of all nations, baptizing them in the name of the Father and of the Son and of the Holy Spirit, ²⁰ and teaching them to obey everything I have commanded you"* (Matthew 28:19-20- New Living Translation).

This was true of the early church when we examine Peter's sermon, and the believers' response following the day of Pentecost experience recorded in Acts chapter 2. It is still true today. A kindle is always needed in the Kingdom, and that kindle does lead to other kindles in the Kingdom.

# CHAPTER EIGHT

# THE RELATIONSHIP BETWEEN PENTECOSTALISM AND THE HOLINESS MOVEMENT IN BARBADOS

I n the introduction, I suggested that the Pentecostal Movement was contemporaneous with the Holiness Movement and that the major characteristics of the Holiness Movement were perpetuated by the Pentecostal Movement. The Pentecostal Movement, therefore, shared a unique relationship with the Holiness Movement. In the late 19th Century and early 20th Century, the Pentecostal Movement drew much of its membership and nearly all of its leadership from Holiness ranks. In this chapter, I review that relationship and make some observations about Pentecostalism and the Holiness Movement in Barbados as seen more specifically through the Pilgrim Holiness Church. Given the nature of the Pentecostal-Holiness relationship, this book would be incomplete without some consideration of it. What were the features of Pentecostalism, and how were these reflective of the nineteenth century Holiness movement? To answer this question, we must consider the theological roots of Pentecostalism. To a committed Pentecostal, it may be Acts Chapter Two; to the missiological student, it may be the Second Awakening or the Holiness revival. Careful reading of the literature does demonstrate actual historical links between Pentecostalism and the Wesleyan Holiness revival of the nineteenth century. Methodism and the broader Evangelical Revival were the major sources of the conversion-oriented piety that found later expression in Pentecostalism. On this score, one needs to be cautious since one cannot easily collapse Methodist and Pentecostal doctrines of conversion. The fact that a great variety of Christian claims can be attributed to John Wesley is a point worth bearing in mind when discussing theological roots of these denominations that emerged out of the Holiness revival. Pentecostalism shares many liturgical practices and theological orientation with the Holiness movement.

The *Dictionary of Pentecostal and Charismatic movements* explained that:

> "Pentecostalism sprang not only from tensions
> between the established Methodist leaders of the

National Holiness Association and their radical, independent Holiness brethren, but also from the commitment to Wesleyan perfectionism, which united them. Perfect love, both groups taught, was both a Methodist doctrine and a Bible doctrine."[139]

Given this commitment to perfectionism, what it is that will distinguish the Pentecostal believer from the Holiness believer? Donald Dayton[140] suggests that the "new" in Pentecostalism, especially over against its immediate predecessors, cannot be denied. However, he warns against allowing this "newness" to preclude the effort to gain a better historical understanding of the emergence of the theological and doctrinal claims of the movement. This caution by Dayton is particularly relevant, for the starting point of the story of Pentecostal roots is not immediately obvious.

Robert Anderson in *Vision of the Disinherited* quotes from a doctrinal statement adopted at the First General Holiness

---

[139] Stanley M. Burgess and Gary B. McGee (eds.) Dictionary of Pentecostal and Charismatic Movements, Grand Rapids, Michigan: Zondervan Publishing House, 1988. 406.

[140] Donald Dayton, Theological Roots of Pentecostalism. The Scarecrow Press, Inc. 1987.36.

Assembly held in Chicago in May 1885. This statement reflects the "orthodox" position on sanctification held by Holiness adherents. It is on the doctrine of "sanctification" that lies much of the theological distinction between Pentecostalism and the Holiness branch. The doctrinal statement read:

> "Entire sanctification more commonly designated as 'sanctification,' 'holiness,' 'Christian perfection,' or 'perfect love,' represents that second definite stage in Christian experience wherein, by the baptism with the Holy Spirit, administered by Jesus Christ, and received instantaneously by faith, the justified believer is delivered from inbred sin, and consequently is saved from all unholy tempers, cleansed from all moral defilement, made perfect in love and introduced into full and abiding fellowship with God."[141]

Anderson further suggested that a rival view, which is most closely associated with the English Keswick movement, split the American Holiness Movement.[142] The Keswick movement gave the doctrine of baptism in the Holy Spirit a different

---

[141] Robert Mapes Anderson. <u>Vision of the Disinherited, The Making of American Pentecostalism,</u> New York: Oxford University Press, 1979. 39.

[142] Ibid. pg. 39.

meaning from that held by the Holiness movement. Anderson contended:

> "They rejected the 'orthodox' Holiness contention that sanctification and Baptism in the Holy Spirit were one and the same experience. Rather, they believed sanctification to be a life-long process of increasing growth in grace that began at conversion but was never completed, and held that the Baptism in the Spirit was a separate 'enduement of power'. At first, there was some uncertainty over whether the Baptism in the Spirit was a second act of grace or a gradual process marked by successive 'fillings' of the Spirit, but the latter view finally prevailed."[143]

The doctrine of Baptism in the Holy Spirit is at the heart of the differences in the Holiness movement. The Wesleyan wing held that Baptism and sanctification are one and the same second act of grace, primarily designed to resolve the problem of sin in the believer. However, there are differences in this wing over whether sanctification is instantaneous and complete or progressive and incomplete. On the other hand, the

---

[143] Ibid. pg. 41.

Keswick wing distinguished between sanctification; which was regarded as a gradual and incomplete process which begins at conversion, and the Baptism in the Spirit, which was an enduement of power. Similar to the Wesleyan wing, there are differences over whether the Baptism was a second act of grace or a process.

One of Robert Anderson's major contentions is that the Keswick movement was very crucial to the development of Pentecostalism. He argued that:

> "That wing of the Pentecostal movement which had earlier connections with Wesleyanism became Pentecostal by accepting Keswick (i.e. Calvinist) teachings on dispensationalism, pre-millennialism and the Baptism of the Holy Spirit. This acceptance led logically to their ostracism of the "orthodox Wesleyan Holiness movement, which held them guilty of the 'Third Blessing heresy.' The majority of Pentecostals were entirely consistent when they later rejected the Wesleyan view of sanctification as a second act of grace."[144]

---

[144] Ibid. pg. 43.

The force of Anderson's argument is clear when he concludes that:

"In short, the Pentecostal movement was as much a departure from the Wesleyan tradition as a development from it."[145]

Donald Dayton also attempts a distinction between the Holiness and Pentecostal camps:

"Holiness Churches, largely a product of the Methodist tradition, follow those who in the ethos of the 19th century camp meeting preserved a variation of the Wesleyan doctrine of 'Christian perfection', emphasizing a post conversion experience of 'entire sanctification'. Distinctly 'Holiness' churches do not speak in tongues; they are among the sharpest critics of the practice. Pentecostal churches teach that Pentecost is a repeatable experience available to Christians in all ages and usually that its appropriation is-'evidenced' by speaking in tongues."[146]

---

[145] Ibid. pg. 43.

[146] Donald W. Dayton in "The Holiness and Pentecostal Churches: Emerging from Cultural Isolation" in Martin E. Martz (ed.), Where the Spirit Leads: American Denominations Today, Atlanta: John Knox Press -1980. 81-82.

Dayton further argues that the Holiness Churches empha-size the "graces" or "fruits" of the Spirit, whereas the Pentecostals emphasize the "gifts" of the Spirit, especially "divine healing" and "glossolalia." This is an interesting distinction that has great merit. "Glossolalia" has certainly been the issue to which various Wesleyan family of Churches have been closed. In addition, the Holiness Movement has had a history involving extreme forms of emotional expression. Many of these were accompanied by "tongues speaking" and in some cases extremist teachings. The memories of these excesses have caused great fear among "ortho-dox" Holiness people. Robert Anderson puts it rather convinc-ingly stating that the rise of the Pentecostal Movement must be seen against the background of a Holiness Movement riven with controversy over the bounds of "liberty in the Spirit".[147]

While discussing the Holiness background of American Pentecostalism, Anderson cites a number of examples of these "excesses":

> "The scenes of torrid emotionalism in the meet-ings of the Holiness evangelist Mrs. Mary B. Woodworth- Etter were typical of the Holiness movement, and increasingly so in the 1890s. The pages of Mrs. Woodworth-Etter's memoirs teem

---

[147] Anderson op.cit. 34.

with references to the most extraordinary 'manifestations of the Spirit.' In a Methodist church in Willshire, Ohio, in 1880 people 'came to the altar screaming for mercy', at another in Monroeville, Indiana, in 1883, 'the aged sisters fell prostrate and became cold and rigid as if dead.'"[148]

It is not surprising that Mrs. Woodworth-Etter became a leading light in the Pentecostal movement.

"By the time she returned to St. Louis fourteen years later, she said, speaking in tongues had assumed greater proportions. A Swedish woman spoke in 'many different languages', one 'sister' sang in Greek and Latin, another spoke in eight different languages, and a 'brother' spoke in three languages, 'sang in the spirit, and laughed in a manner resembling the laughter of several other nations.'"[149]

This example from the early 20th century is also a helpful look at the "perceived" excesses:

"At a Holiness camp meeting in the Arroyo Mountains in 1905, Bartleman complained of the

---

[148] Ibid. pg. 34.
[149] Ibid. pg. 35.

'evanescent froth and foam...religious ranting and bombast.'" Summing up the sentiments of many within and without the Holiness Movement, Bartleman said, "We had a tremendous lot of fanaticism in the Holiness Movement."[150]

The "Pentecostal-Holiness" relationship is also seen at the level of ministry development. It must be remembered that Holiness and Pentecostal churches have been involved in various mergers in the 20th century. Groups like the Church of the Nazarene and the Assemblies of God were built up by a complex process. Various independent ministries, small groups, and local or state associations came together in merger.[151] Timothy L. Smith writing about the organization of the Nazarene Church in the Southeastern part of the United States alludes to the contribution of Pentecostal missions:

> "County holiness associations and holiness unions as well as local units of the Pentecostal Mission provided nuclei for Nazarene congregations."[152]

---

[150] Ibid. pg. 36.

[151] Dayton (1980) op.cit. 94-96.

[152] Timothy L. Smith, <u>Called Unto Holiness, The Story of the Nazarenes: The Formative Years</u>, Kansas City, Missouri: Nazarene Publishing House, 1983. 197.

## PENTECOSTALISM AND MISSIONS

What was the relationship of Pentecostalism and missions? This relationship was a unique one linked to Pentecostals theological emphasis on glossolalia. In Chapters Four and Five, I suggested that in the Holiness Movement there is a relationship between holiness and missions. On the other hand, there is a relationship between speaking in tongues and missions. Many of the early Pentecostals believed that speaking in tongues had a unique missionary function. When the Pentecostal Movement emerged at the beginning of the 20th Century, many people felt called to overseas evangelism. Gary B. McGee contents that:

> "The early records of the revival speak of a close and abiding association between the baptism in the Holy Spirit as evidenced by speaking in tongues for an enduement of power in Christian witness, a fervent belief in the premillennial return of Christ and His command to evangelize to the uttermost parts of the world."[153]

His thesis is that the history of Pentecostalism cannot be properly understood apart from its missionary vision. One

---

[153] L. Grant McClung, Jr. (ed.) <u>Azusa Street and Beyond; Pentecostal Missions and Church Growth in 20th Century</u> Haven: Bridge Publishing Inc. 33

could argue that the Pentecostal movement had the same mission emphasis as the Holiness movement. Both saw missions as necessary and consistent with Biblical faith. Harry Boer[154] contended that from the early days, the Pentecostal experience led to a thrust into missions. From the Pentecostal perspective the Holy Spirit is the chief actor and driving force in missions. Like the Holiness missionaries, Pentecostal missionaries came to the Caribbean islands during the early 20th Century. Because the Pentecostal Movement owes its inspiration and formation to the Holiness Movement, it may be sometimes difficult to make a distinction between Holiness missionaries and Pentecostal missionaries. By Pentecostal missionaries I refer here to those that came out of the Church of God (Cleveland, Tennessee). The Church of God (Cleveland, Tennessee) has the distinction of being North America's oldest Pentecostal denomination.[155] Throughout its history, it has been characterized by a strong missions' emphasis. It has repeatedly sought to maintain a focus on evangelism and world missions. As mentioned in Chapter Four, this church is called the New Testament Church of God in the Caribbean islands. The Caribbean islands were the first location for foreign missionaries from the Church of

---

[154] Harry Boer. <u>Pentecost and Mission</u>. Grand Rapids Eerdsmans, 1964.

[155] Ibid. pg. 170.

God (Cleveland, Tennessee). It began with the Bahamas in 1910 and Jamaica in 1918. The *World Christian Encyclopedia* cites 1917 as the beginning of the New Testament Church of God in Barbados. It is classified as a Pentecostal church and one of the two largest churches in the island.[156]

The Pentecostal Assemblies of the World, commissioned by the Azusa Street experience started mission work around the world from its early years. Roswith I. H. Gerloff, writing on the Black Church Movement in Britain and its transatlantic cultural and theological interaction, argued the following:

> "Foreign mission trips of American PAW officials in the early years of the organization were very rare, perhaps also for financial reasons. Jamaica benefitted most by being geographically near, and was visited among others by Bishop Haywood and Susan G. Lightford in 1931, and by S.N. Hancox and Sanuel Grimes in 1939. Only in the late sixties onward, these travels were extended to Haiti, the Windward Islands and Africa. By the time the PAW had also established itself in other countries such as the Bahamas, Barbados,

---

[156] David Barrett (ed.) <u>World Christian Encyclopedia;</u> Oxford University Press, 1982. 458.

Ghana, Sierra Leone, Egypt, China, India, Israel, Japan, the Philippines, and England."[157]

In her examination of religion and culture, Gerloff admitted that the Pentecostal groups imported from North America have all found an ideal breeding ground in the Caribbean. **What factors explain this reception of Pentecostal Churches?** Several sociological factors came together to explain this proliferation. The socio-economic conditions at the time alluded to previously, were no doubt significant. Among the working class there was a need for hope, a search for identity, not just personal but social and cultural. The Pentecostal message provided Jesus as an "ego-ideal," a hope for the hopeless, a power for the powerless, a fulfillment for the deprived. Pentecostalism therefore had an intrinsic appeal to Caribbean people. It was a force for spiritual sustenance and survival. In his discussion of the lower classes' use of religion in the Caribbean, Kortright Davis pointed out:

"There was a distinct way in which the lower classes took hold of the religion for themselves and gave it a social relevance and efficacy for

---

[157] Roswith I. H. Gerloff. A Plea for British Black Theologies: The Black Church Movement in Britain in its Transatlantic Cultural and Theological Interaction. Frankfurt am Main: Peter Lang, 1992. 119.

which the missionaries could take no credit. Their concepts of sin and divine grace often diverged from the concepts held out to them; God was not a distinct deity, but a very present help in all circumstances. Their songs and daily rituals reflected a close allegiance to a divine presence that could be relied on. Thus while they often found little affirmation in the established churches, they sustained mutual support and assurances among themselves elsewhere."[158]

# SOCIO-ECONOMIC CONDITIONS

One is reminded here of Jesus' announcement of his public ministry. His declaration is a declaration of hope. Hope is the expectation of good; a favorable and confident expectation; joyful and confident expectation of eternal salvation (*Strong's Exhaustive Concordance of the Bible*). His message is a message of hope for the poor and disenfranchised, hope for those who are distressed physically, emotionally, psychologically, socially, culturally and economically. The gospel does in fact create hope.

---

[158] Davis Kortright. <u>Emancipation still Comin': Explorations in Caribbean Emancipatory Theology.</u> Mary Knoll: Orbis Books, 1990. 46.

*"The Spirit of the LORD is upon me, for he has anointed me to bring Good News to the poor. He has sent me to proclaim that captives will be released, that the blind will see, that the oppressed will be set free."* (Luke 4:18 - New Living Translation).

It has been suggested that Pentecostalism is generally associated with the lower classes.[159] This seems to hold true in the case of its development in Barbados at the turn of the 20th century.

There were no social differences between Pentecostals and Pilgrim Holiness believers in Barbados. Both Churches attracted working class people. The style of worship in these churches with an emphasis on singing, collective emotion, informality and participation in worship not only provided an emotional outlet but freedom from a heavy ecclesiastical machine. On the other hand, the mainline churches tended to be reserved and "proper" in their style of worship. However, the absence of restrictions on emotionalism and "the move of the Spirit" was a major difference between the Pentecostal Church and the Pilgrim Holiness Church.

---

[159] See Wilson Bryan. Religious Sects: A Sociological Study. New York: McGraw Hill Book Company, World University Library, 1970 and Simpson George Eaton. "Religions of the Caribbean." In The African Diaspora: Interpretative Essays, edited by Martin L. Kilson and Robert I. Rotberg. Cambridge, Mass. 1976.

It is against this background that I comment on the relationship between the Pilgrim Holiness Church and Pentecostalism in Barbados during the early period of its missions. Oral sources suggest that there was no real relationship. Pentecostals were held in suspicion. Pilgrim Holiness adherents in Barbados were advised against attending Pentecostal meetings or associating with them. Pilgrims saw themselves as more established and conservative than their "glossolalia-centered" counterparts. Pentecostals were seen as being on the fringe of the evangelical movement. This "hands off" attitude among Pilgrims in Barbados was a result of their fear of excesses given what had been experienced in the movement in the United States. Rev.Ives, writing about the Sergeant Village Church, Christ Church, in 1929, referred to the village rather disparagingly as a hotbed of "tongues." He felt that it needed the four-fold gospel in its purity and power and wanted to begin the work of the Church on straight Second Blessing Lines. The one particular experience to which the leadership within the Pilgrim Holiness Church was closed or resistant is the ability to speak and worship God in tongues as the spirit gives utterance. In the United States, the Wesleyan Holiness tradition's rejection of glossolalia, in the wake of the Azusa Street revival of 1906, resulted in the straining of relationships among many former coworkers. In Barbados, the attitude of the Pilgrim Holiness

Church was therefore a major restraining influence on emotional expression, an attempt to tighten the reins on Holiness teachings. All this led to a trend toward increased organization and regulation. The merger with the Wesleyan Methodist Church in 1968 certainly brought that organizational structure to the denomination.

Despite the early suspicion, Pentecostals later became more tolerable. Today, they are finally a part of the contemporary Evangelical group in Barbados. Interchurch relations have certainly been improved. The respectability with which Pentecostalism gradually developed in Barbados must be seen within the wider context of global trends. During the last sixty years, there has been a qualitative and quantitative change in Pentecostalism across the globe. From a qualitative perspective, outstanding shifts in the evaluation of Pentecostals by other Christians have occurred.

Recent history has seen the growing appreciation of the work of the Holy Spirit among some Evangelical groups and a greater appreciation of that Pentecostal tradition. Beginning early in the 1980s, church historians have identified a surge or "wave" of the spirit which has been referred to as "the third wave." Its adherents are primarily evangelicals who heretofore did not want to identify with either the Pentecostal or the Charismatic Movements. These third wave participants, while viewing themselves as neither Pentecostal nor charismatic, suggest that they are simply open to the moving of the Holy Spirit. Given this, and the rapid numerical growth of the two-thirds World, it has become the largest renewal Christian phenomenon of the 20th Century.

The term "Two-Thirds World" was coined in the late 1960s to refer to those non-Western parts of the world formerly referred to as the "Third World" or as the "developing nations." These are the countries of Africa, Asia, Latin America and Oceania. The "Two-Thirds World" is a departure from the traditional stereotypes that some areas of the world were "first" and other parts were "third." The term "first" world reflects a kind of ethnocentrism and cultural imperialism. In the 1980s missiologists and Christian missionaries began using the term "Two-Thirds World". Of significance is the fact that the majority of the world's Christians and the majority of the world's population live in the "Two-Thirds World." Following the 2004 Forum for World Evangelization, the term "majority world church" was recommended to be used instead.

Today the Wesleyan (Pilgrim) Holiness Church in Barbados sees itself as Evangelical, falling into the "neither Pentecostal nor charismatic" group. Many of its adherents are open to the moving of the Holy Spirit, while at the ecclesiastical and theological level "glossolalia" remains a thorny issue and is still not openly encouraged by the leadership. It is, however, embraced by individual believers across the Church District. The issue of continuity and discontinuity is therefore of relevance in the discussion of the relationship between Pentecostalism and the Holiness Movement in Barbados. One wonders about the existence of a direct continuity with the holiness doctrine as taught by Wesley and the Holiness movement. Among some Wesleyans there is evidence of doctrinal modifications especially around the issue of "glossalalia," spiritual gifts and the Baptism with the Holy Spirit. Many younger converts of the Wesleyan Holiness Church are more "charismatic" in orientation, having less of an allegiance to a traditional Wesleyan position. The influence of Pentecostalism in a broader sense must not be overlooked.

The Wesleyan Holiness Church in Barbados must therefore be understood within this new paradigm. The global influence of Pentecostalism, and the charismatic and other church movements on the contemporary church, must not be underestimated. This helps in an understanding, not only of the contemporary Wesleyan Holiness Church but contemporary Evangelical climate within Barbadian society, and the Caribbean community.

# CHAPTER NINE

# A CRITICAL EVALUATION: THE CHURCH AND CARIBBEAN MISSIONS

I n this chapter, I summarize my impressions of the research literature and offer a critical evaluation with a view to the lessons that may be derived for the Church and Caribbean missions. I use the following criteria to evaluate the story that has been told in the preceding chapters:

(1)  Growth

(2)  Relevance and its application to Caribbean missions.

Both growth and relevance are important.

## GROWTH

Measuring the development of the church merely in terms of numerical growth, does not give a total picture of the church's obedience to its mission. Numerical growth does not mean spiritual vibrancy or vitality and is therefore not an obvious indication of church health. Numerical growth can be misleading for it can lull the church in to a false sense of missional complacency. All swelling is not healthy.

## RELEVANCE AND APPLICATION

Relevance and application imply a relationship between mission strategy and the mission field. That relationship is appropriate as the major determinant of relevance. All mission strategy must be contextualized and be therefore relevant to the social, economic and political climate of the mission field, as well as the cultural context and needs of the people to whom the mission is targeted. Invariably, relevance without growth is meaningless.

The history of the Wesleyan Holiness Church in Barbados is a fascinating story of the witness of holiness missionaries and local believers. Inspired leadership, creativity and sacrificial service were characteristic of that witness. The research in the preceding chapters reveals the following:

(1) The Holiness Movement provided the ground out of which important advances in missions took place in the late nineteenth and early twentieth centuries in the Caribbean islands.

(2) These missions were primarily North American missions and significantly mirrored the North American evangelical scene at the time.

The Holiness movement was indeed one of the significant renewal movements in the history of the Protestant Church. With this in mind, one can postulate that there is **a causal relationship between spiritual renewal and mission**, a relationship that was evident in the growth of the Wesleyan Holiness Church in Barbados. As we assess that relationship, we need to ask ourselves two questions:

(1) What was the theory of missions?
(2) Did the theory (if it existed) determine the missionary strategy?

It is the answers to these questions that help us to evaluate relevance.

Careful analysis of the evangelization suggests that there was no clearly defined theory of missions. No theory informed the missions of Methodist or the Wesleyan Holiness Church in Barbados. However, the sense of missions was clearly rooted in a vital experience of scriptural holiness. Because of the perception of spiritual need, the island of Barbados was looked to as a mission field. In terms of missions' strategy, the main object of missions was the establishment of the Church in the island. Among the missionaries, there was a vigorous attempt to establish mission stations in every parish on the island. One repeated method used was the open-air or street meeting. This was true for the work of Holiness groups like the Salvation Army, the Nazarenes and the Pilgrim Holiness Church in Barbados. Doubtless, the importance of the informal setting was favored. It appropriately connected with the social value of the working class people. In some sense it may have also favored the development of native spiritual leaders. Developing local spiritual leaders is a very important part of foreign missions and church planting.

# THE RELATIONSHIP BETWEEN EVANGELIZATION AND SOCIAL ACTION?

What was the Relationship between Evangelization and Social action? This is an important question for the church and for Christian missions. The church's response to issues of poverty and social justice is an indication of the church's willingness to embrace the heart of Jesus. This is Kingdom work, that is, the work that Christians do in the service of Christ. There is no doubt that the poor are often society's most neglected members. In various parts of the world, people have made some progress in overcoming hunger and addressing issues of poverty. However, in a world where there is more than enough food for all people, ongoing issues of hunger are a disgrace to the church. Our responsibility in this Kingdom work is to respond with compassion in concrete and specific ways, as Jesus would, and as He has called us to do. He instructs us to care for those who are hungry and thirsty, for those who are sick or in prison, for those who are the outcasts of society.

> [34] *"Then the King will say to those on his right, 'Come, you who are blessed by my Father; take your inheritance, the kingdom prepared for you since the creation of the world.* [35] *For I was hungry and you gave me something to eat, I was thirsty and you gave me something to drink, I was a stranger and you invited me in,* [36] *I needed clothes and you clothed me, I was sick and you looked after me, I was in prison and you came to visit me.'*

> [37] *"Then the righteous will answer him, 'Lord, when did we see you hungry and feed you, or thirsty and give you something to drink?* [38] *When did we see you a stranger and invite you in, or needing clothes and clothe you?* [39] *When did we see you sick or in prison and go to visit you?'*

[40] *"The King will reply, 'Truly I tell you, whatever you did for one of the least of these brothers and sisters of mine, you did for me.'* **Matthew 25:34-40 - New International Version (NIV)**

While at the house of a prominent Pharisee on the Sabbath day, Jesus gives some very powerful instructions:

[12] *Then Jesus said to his host, "When you give a luncheon or dinner, do not invite your friends, your brothers or sisters, your relatives, or your rich neighbors; if you do, they may invite you back and so you will be repaid.* [13] *But when you give a banquet, invite the poor, the crippled, the lame, the blind,* [14] *and you will be blessed. Although they cannot repay you, you will be repaid at the resurrection of the righteous."* **Luke 14:12-15 - New International Version (NIV)**

While Holiness missionaries did not come to the island with social programs as a major objective of mission, attempts were made by individual churches to provide food, clothing, and household items to those in need. In addition; there were financial appeals by missionaries to their holiness brethren in North America. The emphasis of missions was, more particularly, spiritual transformation and empowerment as opposed to economic empowerment. To say this, though, is not to suggest that material needs were overlooked. In numerous cases, local believers assisted each other. This was partly a reflection of the collectivism and strong sense of community that was a feature of Barbadian society at the time.

That the Wesleyan Holiness Church in Barbados has grown since the beginning of its missions is evident. By 1929, there were twenty-nine churches with a membership of over twelve hundred. By 1979, the number of churches increased to forty and the membership doubled. While there was a reduction in the rate of growth then, the church has steadily grown both in terms of its "following" and national recognition (image) to become one of the leading Evangelical churches in contemporary Barbadian society. In 2016, the number of churches stands at thirty-eight. The founding of the Church in a new land, and the spread of scriptural holiness as a vital experience in the life of the church, as objects of missions, has definitely been achieved. The Wesleyan tradition is certainly being perpetuated through the Wesleyan Holiness Church in Barbados.

## THREE LAWS OF MISSIONS

In this chapter, I identify three factors shaping missions in Barbados and I derive three "laws" of missions. As used here, the term "law" loosely covers a set of observations that leads to a summative conclusion. The "law" reflects a missiological principle as it relates to the history and nature of missionary work to the Caribbean. These laws have implications for Caribbean missions and provide some ground for theological reflection. Based on the research, it is clear that Christian mission in Barbados was a consequence of three major factors, each reflecting the historical and sociological dynamics of a particular epoch:

(1)  Colonialism
(2)  Evangelism and Social Justice
(3)  Perception of Spiritual Decadence.

## COLONIALISM

Colonialism is part of the history and reality of all Caribbean countries, and is both insidious and synonymous with control. Colonialism determined the emergence of the first Christian missions to the Caribbean and involved the colonial transplanting of the church of the "Mother Country" - Britain. It represented the need to transplant the church of the British Empire in all colonies that Britain had acquired. It is reflected in the dominance of the Anglican Church on the island of Barbados, not only in the 18th Century but in contemporary society. In most of the British West Indian colonies, the Anglican Church was the established church. In Barbados, this dated back from the imposition of British rule in the seventeenth century.

Reflecting similarly on this issue, Stephen Neill examined the relationship between the mission of the church and the aggressive policies of the various nations to which missionaries belonged. He is of the view that missions can be classed as one of the instruments of Western infiltration and control.[160] He further argued that:

> "Missions have constituted a direct threat to those religious institutions on which all ancient cultures are founded, and by which they are held together - the most dangerous of all forms of aggression, since this strikes at the heart of the nations and endangers their very existence as peoples with a history and a destiny."[161]

Indian historian K.M. Panikkar, in his book, *Asia Under Western Domination* argued that there is a close alliance between missions and the physical power of the conquering nations. This led to missions being dangerous. He maintained

---

[160] Neill, Stephen. <u>Colonialism and Christian Mission.</u> New York: McGraw Hill, 1966. 12.

[161] Ibid. pg.12.

that the only notable successes of the missions in Asia at the time were obtained when they could rely on the superior force of the Western nations.[162]

The foregoing perspectives point to a kind of cultural imperialism attendant with colonialism. Christian missions are seen as part of the "package" that accompanied the colonialism of the British Empire. To engage Britain meant a simultaneous engagement of her religion, her ethos and culture in all its forms.

In a well-documented work entitled, The Bible and the Flag, Brian Stanley presents an alternative perspective. He attempts to offer a corrective to the view that accuses Christian missions of allowing themselves to be used as the tools of imperialism and economic exploitation. He acknowledges that the experience of the mission field forced missionaries to adopt a variety of, more or less, explicitly political stances. In reference to Christian missions and slavery in the Caribbean islands, he argued that:

> "Missionary Christianity was not a welcome ally for colonial oppression but a disturbing challenge to it."[163]

---

[162] Panikkar. K.M. Asia Under Western Domination, London, 1952.

[163] Stanley, Brian. The Bible and the Flag: Protestant Missions and British Imperialism in the 19th and 20th Centuries. Leicester, England: Apollos, 1990.90.

## EVANGELISM AND SOCIAL JUSTICE

Evangelism and Social justice characterized the period of the 18th and 19th Centuries. It was evident in the work of the Moravians, as well as Methodist and Baptist missionaries, and represented the need to Christianize the slaves and address social injustices. It was linked to the historical debates in Britain on the status of the slave system at the time.

## PERCEPTION OF SPIRITUAL DECADENCE

In the early 20th Century, given the perceived spiritual and social conditions in Barbados, it was believed that there was a need for revival and "holiness living." This represented the work of Holiness missionaries and particularly the Wesleyan (Pilgrim) Holiness missions.

In assessing the work of Christian missions, one must remember, as noted earlier, that wherever a Colonial power went (to colonize), she took her institutions, the church being one of these. This pattern of Colonial dominance is sufficiently evident to embolden me to state my **first "law" of missions**: **<u>There is a relationship between political history and mission strategy.</u>** Geopolitical considerations help shape missions. It is not surprising that by the late 19th Century, and turn of the 20th Century there was an influx of North American Holiness missions into Barbados and other islands. Although the reasons for this are subject to debate, one could argue that at some level, it reflected a change in "masters." The islands moved from the Colonial dominance of Britain, following the decline of sugar and achievement of slave emancipation, to the prominence of the United States as an economic and political "watchdog" to the Caribbean region. It is true to say that by the 20th Century, Britain had been replaced by the "superpower to the North" – the United States of America. Consequently, America's political and economic influence in the region grew. It is my contention, that here America's 19th century "Manifest Destiny" was repackaged and perpetuated. One cannot separate the practice of American missionary enterprise from the policy of American Expansionism. These two have always gone together, even on the continent of North America. The examples of Oregon and Hawaii in the 19th Century were both examples of "foreign missions" that were domesticated. **Religion and politics do indeed mix.**

In terms of missions and colonialism, Stephen Neill[164] suggested that the subject is highly complex. Its contours vary from period to period and from area to area. It varies in accordance with the policies of the various countries concerned in the

---

[164] Stephen Neill (1966)

colonial enterprise. Neill points appropriately to the need for caution and restraint, and the difficulty in making generalizations. When made, these generalizations should be put forward only in tentative fashion.

The work of the Pilgrim Holiness missions in Barbados and the growth of the Wesleyan Holiness Church suggest **a second "law" of missions**: **It is impossible to separate holiness from missions.** The two are interrelated and interdependent. Undesirable socioeconomic and spiritual conditions encourage reflection on scriptural holiness which propels missions. It seems to me that an evangelical concern for the advance of the gospel is largely related to some concern about right or holy living. This focus on holiness seems to provide a challenge for Christian missions; hence the nature of the relationship between holiness and missions is a catalytic one. These observations lead to **my third "law" of missions**: **Vibrant mission strategy is a product of spiritual renewal.** The relationship is often a reciprocal one, but not always even and consistent. The missiological study presented in this book embodies this third law. Outside of this, the Biblical account of the early Church and the specific periods of the Reformation in the history of the Church, are also testimony to this great truth. Throughout the history of the Church several great steps in missions were linked to an intense spirituality. Following the upper room experience in Acts 2, the early church saw a vibrancy that led to missions.

> [38] Peter replied, "Repent and be baptized, every one of you, in the name of Jesus Christ for the forgiveness of your sins. And you will receive the gift of the Holy Spirit. [39] The promise is for you and your children and for all who are far off—for all whom the Lord our God will call." [40] With many other words he warned them; and he pleaded with them, "Save yourselves from this corrupt generation." [41] Those who accepted his message were baptized, and about three thousand were added to their number that day. **Acts 2:38-41 - New International Version (NIV).**

Missionary concern goes hand in hand with spiritual renewal. The strong missionary orientation of the Holiness Movement may be explained perhaps because it (the Holiness Movement) arose during the great century of Christian missions, and perhaps because of the influence of Acts 1:8 which conjoin the power of the Holy Spirit with witnessing to the ends of the earth. The importance of pneumatological issues in missions must therefore be recognized.

The relationship between spirituality and Christian missions has also been suggested by the observations of missiologist Samuel Escobar.[165] Writing on popular Protestantism in Latin America, Escobar acknowledged that Popular Protestantism is a movement that mobilizes people for mission. It has a remarkable ability to mobilize all members of their churches for missionary task. He argues that it could well be the movement that carries the seeds for the reformation and completion of Christian mission in Latin America and from there to other parts of the world.[166] Although the existence of a theory of missions in the missiological study presented in this book is subject to conjecture, one could argue that missionary strategy and methods tended to point to theory as opposed to a strategy emerging out of a theory. While there was no espoused theory, there seems to have been underlying realities shaping missions - these are political, social, economic and theological.

---

[165] See J. Samuel Escobar, "Conflict of Interpretations of Popular Protestantism" in Guilleumo Cook, Ed.New Face of the Church in Latin America. Orbis Books, 1994 and J. Samuel Escobar, "The Promise and Precariousness of Latin American Protestantism" in Daniel R. Miller, ed. Coming of Age, University Press of America, 1994.

[166] J. Samuel Escobar, "Conflict of Interpretations of Popular Protestantism" pg.112.

# CHAPTER TEN

# IMPLICATIONS FOR CARIBBEAN MISSIONS AND THEOLOGICAL REFLECTION

W hat then are the implications of the *Kindle in the Kingdom* for Caribbean missions? What was discovered in presenting these models was that the social, economic, cultural and political context of the islands account a great deal for the nature and style of Christian missions. There are a few challenges. Firstly, any Christian missions in the Caribbean must begin with an analysis of the community. The political and economic realities of the times must be taken into account. This is true even for Regional Missions (island to island). The territory of Guyana, a Caribbean territory on the coast of South America, is a case in point. Here the economic realities are products of the sociopolitical culture of the society. Guyana as a mission field is "ripe" and this is related to economic realities of its people. It seems that when people are oppressed, either economically, socially or politically, religion becomes a kind of liberation. Missionary work prospers most in oppressed conditions. The story of Holiness missions in Barbados is testimony to this.

The message of Christian missions must help people to find their own identity out of a broken and fragmented past. It is then that we are engaged in theological reflection. I use the term "theological reflection" to refer to critical reflection on the meaning of life -on the meaning of God, self, others and the environment. What is the function of religion in the Caribbean is a major part of that reflection. Secondly, any attempt at Caribbean missions must bear in mind the function of religion in the Caribbean context. In the words of Roswith Gerloff, "religion is the substance of culture, and culture is the form of religion. [167] Religion in the Caribbean helps people to come to grips with the problems they need to solve. It gives them a certain degree of autonomy, which allows them to function amidst their current realities.

---

[167] Roswith Gerloff, <u>A Plea for British Black Theologies, The Black Church Movement in Britain in Its Transatlantic Cultural and Theological</u>, Frankfurt am Main: Peter Lang, 1992. 140.

This phenomenon seems to express similarly in Africa, Asia and Latin America. The 2004 Forum for World Evangelization hosted by the Lausanne Committee for World Evangelization observed a significant shift in the global Church with the former so called "third World" countries showing an increased large number of Christians. In a paper highlighting *"The Two-Thirds World Church and Evangelization"* it was pointed out that:

> "While one hundred years ago 95% of Christians lived in the western world, nowadays 70% of believers live in Africa, Asia and Latin America. The most dynamic and growing churches are in this part of the world." [168]

This is significant because **not o**nly is this part of the world seen as poorer, but this part of the world have two-thirds of the world's population, and also two-thirds of the world's Christians.

The third challenge to Caribbean missions has to do with spiritual renewal. If we accept that missions are a product of

---

[168] Lausanne Committee for World Evangelization <u>A New Vision, a New Heart, a Renewed Call. Lausanne Occasional Paper No. 44</u>. The 2004 Forum for World Evangelization, Pattaya, Thailand: September 29th to October 5th, 2004

spiritual renewal, then what are the social, economic and political realities, including historical antecedents of the Caribbean that should inform and challenge the development of spiritual renewal? What guidance can we gain from the experience of the Wesleyan (Pilgrim) Holiness missions in Barbados? In discerning that, we must be clear as to the diffusion of missionary influence over wide areas as opposed to its concentration in strategic points. The strategic areas of interest in the Caribbean must be identified.

A further response to the contemporary realities of the Caribbean is a serious consideration of the elements of a "social Gospel." While one should not attempt to spread missions by direct offer of material inducements, it seems to me, that the need to consider the economic realities of the people is paramount in developing a vibrant, relevant and sustaining mission strategy. As discussed earlier, the gospel must affect not only the emotional and spiritual areas of people's lives, but the totality of who they are as well.

A fourth challenge to Caribbean missions is that of growth. The experience of the Pilgrim Holiness missions discussed in this book suggests that traditional methods of missions - open-air, tent meetings, cottage meetings - were critical to the growth and development of the mission in Barbados. While still effective in their own right, it seems to me, that any mission strategy must now consider the educational realities of the people. On a whole, the fact is that the masses of the Caribbean are certainly more educated and informed than their foreparents in the early part of the 20th Century. What I am suggesting is that education must be an important consideration in mission planning. Mission planning must also consider the impact of globalization on the world and on the Church. At a time when the world has become a "global village," current mission strategy must wisely consider ways to effectively and creatively use modern day media and technology to enhance and support the work of mission. The Evangelical Churches in the Caribbean region share a common history and theological heritage. In this context, greater dialogue should be favorable. Growth through merger may be a viable consideration for missions. Merging with compatible denominations is one of the best ways for the Christian community to extend its influence and witness to the unity of the Body of Christ. The experience of the Pilgrim Holiness Missions suggests this as a prospect worth exploration and reflection.

While many churches in the Caribbean may no longer be in a strictly "missionary situation," there is need for missionary consolidation. It must be acknowledged that great ecumenical progress has been made in the Caribbean Church; however, the need for churches to come together in the spirit of cooperation is still apparent. Mission strategy within the Caribbean must seek to prepare both old and new believers to be agents of transformation in their own communities.

Caribbean people have a number of positive factors to rely on as they confront these challenges. The collective will of the people, the quality of their resilience, the value of freedom and dignity, the experience of the consolation of God in their pain and suffering, to name a few, are all valuable. To respond to these challenges is therefore to answer the longing of the Caribbean Church for relevance, identity, justice, and hope as it responds to the call of God to the people in the region. The major task of theological reflection in Caribbean Missions, then, is to understand how the people have experienced God in the past and how they make that relevant to their contemporary situation. Caribbean people must be able to tell their story, and the gospel must be used to help people make sense of their story and embrace the essential redemptive truth of that gospel. Theological reflection in Caribbean Missions must also engender a reaffirmation of the value of Christian community in a post-Christian technological age. When these are maintained, the Caribbean islands will continue to be a kindle in the Kingdom.

# BIBLIOGRAPHY

BOOKS:

Ahlstrom, Sydney E. <u>A Religious History of the American People.</u> New Haven: Yale University Press, 1972.

Allen, Roland. The Spontaneous Expansion of the Church. Grand Rapids: Eerdmans, 1962.

Allen, Roland. <u>Missionary Methods: St. Paul's or Ours?</u> London: World Dominion Press, 1953.

Anderson, Robert Mapes. <u>Vision of the Disinherited, the Making of American Pentecostalism.</u> New York: Oxford University Press, 1979.

Bakke, Ray., and Jim Hart. <u>The Urban Christian: Effective Ministry in Today's Urban World.</u> Downers Grove: InterVarsity Press, 1987.

151

Beardsley, Frank Grenville. The History of Christianity in America. New York: American Tract Society, 1938.

Blackman, Francis. Methodism: 200 Years in Barbados. Bridgetown, Barbados: Caribbean Contact Ltd., 1988.

Bloch-Hoell, Nils. The Pentecostal Movement, Its Origin, Development and Distinctive Character. Oslo and London, 1964.

Boer, Harry R. Pentecost and Mission. Grand Rapids: Eerdmans, 1964.

Bosch, David J. Transforming Mission: Paradigm Shifts in Theology of Mission. Mary Knoll: Orbis, 1991.

Bossard, Johann Jacob. History of the Mission of the Evangelical

Brethren on the Caribbean islands of St. Thomas, St. Croix and St. John. Karoma Publishers, Inc., 1987.

Bruce, F. F. Paul: Apostle of the Heart Set Free. Grand Rapids, Eerdsmans, 1977.

Bucke, Emory Stevens, ed., <u>The History of American Methodism Volume 1.</u> New York: Abingdon Press, 1964.

Cameron, Richard W. <u>The Rise of Methodism: A Source Book.</u> New York: Philosophical Library, 1954.

Cavit, Marshall. <u>The Will of my Father: Messages on the Relation- ship Between Holiness and Missions.</u> Newberg, Oregon: The Barclay Press, 1968.

Conn, Harvie. Eternal Word and Changing Worlds: Theology, Anthropology and Mission in Trialogue. Grand Rapids, Zondervan, 1984.

Cook, Guillermo, ed. New Face of the Church in Latin America. Mary Knoll: Orbis Books, 1994.

Coote, Robert., and John Stott., eds. <u>Down to Earth, Studies in Christianity and Culture.</u> Grand Rapids: Eerdmans, 1980.

Crahan, M. & Franklin Knight (eds.) <u>Africa and the Caribbean, The Legacies of a Link.</u> Baltimore: John Hopkins University Press, 1979.

Cuthbert, Robert W.M. <u>Ecumenism and Development: Socio-historical Analysis of the Caribbean Conference of Churches.</u> Columbia University, 1984.

Davis, Kortright. <u>Emancipation Still Comin': Explorations in Caribbean Emancipatory Theology.</u> Mary Knoll: Orbis Books, 1990.

Davis, Kortright. <u>Mission for Caribbean Change.</u> Frankfurt: Peter Lang, 1982.

Dayton, Donald. <u>Discovering an Evangelical Heritage.</u> New York: Harper and Row, 1976.

Dayton, Donald W. <u>The American Holiness Movement: A Bibliographic Introduction.</u> Wilmore, Kentucky: Asbury Theological Seminary, 1971.

Dayton, Donald. <u>Theological Roots of Pentecostalism.</u> The Scare- crow Press, Inc. 1987.

Dayton, Donald, and Robert Johnston. <u>The Variety of American Evangelicalism.</u> The University of Tennessee Press, 1991.

Dempster Murray A., Byron D. Klaus, Douglas Petersen. <u>Called and Empowered: Global Mission in Pentecostal Perspective.</u> Hendrickson Publishers, Inc., 1991.

Dieter, Melvin E. <u>The Holiness Revival of the Nineteenth Century</u> Metuchen, New Jersey: Scarecrow Press, 1980.

Drummond, Lewis. <u>The Life and Ministry of Charles G. Finney.</u> Minneapolis, Minnesota: Bethany House Publishers, 1983.

Dunn, James D.G., <u>Spirit Baptism and Pentecostalism.</u> Scottish Journal of Theology 23 (Nov. 1990): 397-407.

Edman, V. Raymond. <u>Finney Lives On: The Man, His Revival Methods and His Message.</u> New York: Fleming H. Revell Co., 1951.

Erskine, Noel Leo. <u>Decolonizing Theology: A Caribbean Perspective.</u> Mary Knoll: Orbis Books, 1981.

Fitchett, W.H. <u>Wesley and His Century.</u> London: Smith, Elder and Co., 1951.

Gerloff, Roswith. I.H. <u>A Plea for British Black Theologies: The Black Church Movement in Britain and Its Transatlantic Cultural and Theological Interaction.</u> Frankfurt am Main: Peter Lang, 1992.

Glazier, Stephen D., ed., <u>Perspectives on Pentecostalism: Case Studies from the Caribbean and Latin American.</u> Washington: University Press of America, 1980.

Gonzalez, Justo L. <u>The Development of Christianity in the Latin Caribbean.</u> Grand Rapids, Michigan: Eerdsmans, 1969.

Hamid, Idris ed. <u>Troubling of the Waters.</u> Trinidad: San Fernando, 1973.

Hamid, Idris. <u>Out of the Depths, a Collection of Papers Presented at Four Missiology Conferences, Held in Antigua, Guyana, Jamaica and Trinidad in 1975.</u> San Fernando, Trinidad, 1977.

Hiebert, Paul G. <u>Anthropological Reflections on Missiological Issues.</u> Grand Rapids, Michigan: Baker Books, 1994.

Hinchliff, Peter. <u>Holiness and Politics.</u> Grand Rapids, Michigan: William Eerdmans Publishing Company, 1982.

Hobbs, Doreen. <u>Jewels of the Caribbean, The Story of the Salvation Army in the Caribbean Territory.</u> St. Albans: The Campfield Press, 1986.

Hollenweger, Walter J. <u>The Pentecostals - The Charismatic Movement in the Churches.</u> Minneapolis, Minnesota: Augsburg, 1972.

Horowitz, Michael., ed. <u>Peoples and Cultures of the Caribbean.</u> Garden City, New York, 1971.

Hurst, John Fletcher. <u>History of the Christian Church. Vol. II</u> New York, 1900.

Jones, Charles Edwin. <u>Perfectionist Persuasion, the Holiness Movement and American Methodism,</u> 1867-1936. Metuchen, New Jersey: The Scarecrow Press, 1974.

Kostlevy, William. <u>Holiness Manuscripts: A Guide to Sources Documenting the Wesleyan Holiness Movement in the United States and Canada.</u> Metuchen, N.J.: The Scarecrow Press, Inc., 1994.

LaTourette, Kenneth Scott. <u>A History of the Expansion of Christianity Vols. 3 & 4.</u> Harper and Brothers, 1937-45; Zondervan, 1971.

Laurence K.O. (ed.). <u>A Selection of Papers Presented at the Twelfth Conference of the Association of Caribbean Historians</u> U.W.I. St. Augustine, Trinidad, 1980.

Lewis, Gordon K. <u>Main Currents in Caribbean Thought.</u> Baltimore: John Hopkins University Press, 1983.

Lowenthal, David and Conitas Lambros., eds. <u>Consequences of Class and Color: West Indian Perspectives.</u> New York, 1975.

Martin, David. <u>Tongues of Fire.</u> Oxford: Basil Blackwell, 1980.

Marty, Martin E., ed. <u>Where the Spirit Leads: American Denominations Today.</u> Atlanta, Georgia: John Knox Press, 1980.

McClung, Jr. L. Grant, ed. <u>Azusa Street and Beyond. Pentecostal Missions and Church Growth in the Twentieth Century.</u> Bridge Publishing Inc., 1986.

McKinley, Edward H. <u>Marching to Glory: The History of the Salvation Army in the United States.</u> San Francisco: Harper and Row, 1980.

McLoughlin, William G., ed. <u>Lectures on Revivals of Religion by Charles G. Finney.</u> Cambridge, Massachusetts: The Belkin Press, 1960.

Mead, Frank S. <u>Handbook of Denominations in the United States, New Sixth Edition.</u> New York: Abingdon Press, 1975.

Miller, Basil. <u>Charles G. Finney, He Prayed Down Revivals.</u> Grand Rapids, Michigan: Zondervan, 1941.

Miller, Daniel R., ed. <u>Coming of Age: Protestantism in Contemporary Latin America.</u> University Press of America, 1994.

Myers, Bryant L. <u>The Changing Shape of World Mission.</u> Monrovia: March, 1993.

Neill, Stephen. <u>A History of Christian Missions 2nd Ed.</u> Baltimore: Penguin Books, 1986.

Neill, Stephen. <u>Colonialism and Christian Mission</u>. New York: McGraw Hill, 1966.

Neill, Stephen, ed. <u>Concise Dictionary of the Christian World Mission.</u> Nashville: Abingdon Press, 1971.

Parker, John A. <u>A Church in the Sun: The Story of the Rise of Methodism in the Island of Grenada, West Indies.</u> London: Cargate Press, 1959.

Parkhurst, Jonis Gifford, Jr., ed. <u>Principles of Sanctification Charles G. Finney.</u> Minneapolis, Minnesota: Bethany House, 1986.

Phillips, James M. and Robert T. Coote, eds. <u>Toward the 21st Century in Christian Mission.</u> Grand Rapids: Eerdmans, 1993.

Robinson, Charles Henry. <u>History of Christian Missions.</u> New York: Charles Scribner's Sons, 1915.

Rusk, David. <u>Cities Without Suburbs.</u> Woodrow Wilson Center Press, 1993.

Sanneh, Lamin. <u>Translating the Message The Missionary Impact on Culture.</u> Mary Knoll: Orbis Books, 1989.

Scopes, Wilfred, ed. <u>The Christian Ministry in Latin America and the Caribbean.</u> New York: World Council of Churches, 1962.

Senior, Donald, and Carrol Stuhlmueller. <u>The Biblical Foundations for Mission.</u> Mary Knoll: Orbis Books, 1983.

Smith, Glen, Rachel Smith & Mary Arllie. <u>Caribbean Call: The Missionary Story of Glen and Rachel Smith.</u> Word A Flame Press, 1991.

Smith, Timothy L. <u>Called Unto Holiness, The Story of the Nazarene Formative years.</u> Kansas, Missouri, Nazarene Publishing House, 1962.

Smith, Timothy L. <u>Revivalism and Social Reform in the Mid-Nine- teenth Century America.</u> New York: Abingdon Press, 1957.

Stanley, Brian. <u>The Bible and the Flag - Protestant Missions and British Imperialism in the Nineteenth and Twentieth Centuries.</u> Leicester, England: Apollos, 1990.

Strong, James. <u>Strong's Exhaustive Concordance of the Bible.</u> Hendrickson Publishers, Inc.; Updated edition. April 9, 2009

Sunshine, Catherine A. <u>The Caribbean: Survival, Struggle and Sovereignty.</u> Washington, D.C.: EPICA, 1985.

Tallman, J. Raymond. <u>An Introduction to World Missions.</u> Chicago, Moody Press, 1989.

The Holy Bible: Today's New International Version. 2005.Grand
  Rapids, MI: Zondervan


Tidball, Derek J. Who are the Evangelicals? Tracing the Roots of
  Today's Movements. London: Marshall Pickering, 1994.


Titus, Noel F. The Development of Methodism in Barbados
  1823-1883 Peter Lang, Inc.: European Academic
  Publishers, 1994.


Turk, Mary. Slaves and Missionaries: The Disintegration of
  Jamaican Slave Society 1787-1834. Chicago: University of
  Illinois Press, 1982.


Tyerman, Luke. The Life and Times of Rev. John Wesley. New
  York: Harpers, 1872.


Urlin, R. Denny. John Wesley's Place in Church History.
  London, 1870.


Watson, Jackson, The West Indian Heritage: A History of The
  West Indies. London: John Murray, 1979.

Weddle, David L. <u>The Law As Gospel: Revival and Reform in The Theology of Charles G. Finney.</u> Metuchen, New Jersey: The Scarecrow Press, 1985.

Wilcox, Leslie. <u>Be Ye Holy: A Study of The Teaching of Scripture Relative to Entire Sanctification, With a Sketch of the History and the Literature of the Holiness Movement.</u> Ohio: Revivalist Press, 1965.

Wilson, Bryan. <u>Religious Sects: A Sociological Study.</u> New York: McGraw Hill, 1970.

Wright, Frederick G. <u>Charles Grandson Finney.</u> Boston: The Riverside Press, 1891.

## REFERENCE WORKS

Barrett, David B., ed. <u>World Christian Encyclopedia.</u> New York: Oxford University Press, 1982.

Burgess, Stanley M., and Gary B. McGee., ed. <u>Dictionary of Pentecostal and Charismatic Movements.</u> Grand Rapids, Michigan: Zondervan, 1988.

Neill, Stephan, and Gerald Anderson, John Goodwin. <u>Concise Dictionary of the Christian World Mission.</u> New York: Abingdon Press, 1971.

O'Brien, T.C. ed. <u>Corpus Dictionary of Western Churches.</u> Washington: Corpus Publications, 1970.

Siewart, John, and John Kenyon, eds. <u>Mission Handbook (15th Edition)</u>. Monrovia: MARC, 1993.

## ARTICLES

Handler, Jerome S., and Charlotte Frisbie. "Aspects of Slave Life in Barbados: Music and Its Cultural Context." <u>Caribbean Studies.</u> 11 (4): 5-46, 1972.

Mintz, Sidney W. "The Caribbean Region" Sidney W. Mintz., ed. <u>Slavery Colonialism and Racism.</u> pp. 43-71. New York: N.W. Norton, 1974.

# MAGAZINES

Escobar, Samuel. "Mission in Latin America: An Evangelical Perspective" <u>Missiology</u> XX(2), April 1992: 241-253. <u>The Wesleyan Holiness Advocate.</u> Vol. 6, No. 3, May-June 1980.

# NEWSPAPERS

Davis, Kortright. "Caribbean Emancipation and the Christians Gospel." <u>Caribbean Contact,</u> August 1984.

Granado, Gerard. "Towards a Caribbean Theology." <u>Caribbean Contact,</u> April 1983.

Hamid, Idris. "Caribbean Church" <u>Caribbean Contact,</u> July 1979.

James, Mike. "Towards a Caribbean Theology." <u>Caribbean Contact,</u>April 1983.

# UNPUBLISHED SOURCES

Bend, James E. "Report on Church Growth," Paper submitted to the Forty Third Annual District Conference, Barbados District of Wesleyan Holiness Church. n.d.

"Called to Be," Report of the Caribbean Ecumenical Consultation For Development, 2nd edition. Bridgetown: CADEC, 1973.

Clarke, Knolly, "Ministry in the Decade of the 80s" Lecture delivered at Seminar on Theological Conference of Pastor and Educators. Trinidad 1981. Towards a Caribbean Theology, Caribbean Ecumenical Program.

Cone, James. "What is Christian Theology" delivered at Seminar on Liberation Theology. San Fernando: Trinidad, 1976. Towards a Caribbean Theology, Caribbean Ecumenical Program.

Cupid, John. "Caribbean Culture", paper presented at a Seminar on Youth Work - Study Encounter, 1980. Towards a Caribbean Theology, Caribbean Ecumenical Program.

Godson F. "A Half Century of Ups and Downs in the Eastern West Indies, Reminiscences of Rev. F. Godson, Methodist Minister" Chelsea Cottage, St. Michael. No. 17 4th September 1951.

Hamid, Idris. "Towards a Caribbean Theology" seminar on the Religious Experience of Caribbean people. Trinidad, 1978. <u>Towards a Caribbean Theology,</u> Caribbean Ecumenical Program.

Ives, Wingrove R. "A Missionary's Cry from Barbados." Foreign Missionary Department, Pilgrim Holiness Church, 1929.

Lasanne Committee for World Evangelization<u>A New Vision, a New Heart, a Renewed Call. Lausanne Occasional Paper No. 44</u>. The 2004 Forum for World Evangelization, Pattaya, Thailand: September 29th to October 5th, 2004

Lett, Leslie A. "Third World Theology and Politics." Jubilee Research Centre, 1986.

Rodney Walter "A Survey of Marxist Philosophy" lecture delivered at Seminar on Contemporary Ideologies and Christian Faith.

San Fernando: Trinidad, 1977. <u>Toward a Caribbean Theology,</u> Caribbean Ecumenical Program.

"The Christian Ministry, a New Departure", lecture delivered at the Hilda Prudden Lecture, Nassau, Bahamas, November 1976.

## NON-PRINT SOURCES

Bend, James. Personal Interview. Barbados 10th March 1996.

Gilmore, John. Personal Interview. Barbados 7th March 1996.

Titus, Noel. Personal Interview. Barbados 7th March 1996.

Wesleyan Holiness Church, Barbados. Personal Interviews with Church members, August, 1994.

Williams, Carlisle. Personal Interview. Barbados 6th March 1996.

CPSIA information can be obtained
at www.ICGtesting.com
Printed in the USA
BVHW03s1308220418
513795BV00003B/2/P